Children of the Levee

LAFCADIO HEARN

Children
of the
Levee

Edited by O.W. FROST *Introduction by* JOHN BALL

THE UNIVERSITY OF KENTUCKY PRESS

THE PUBLICATION OF THIS BOOK IS POSSIBLE PARTLY BECAUSE OF A GRANT FROM
THE MARGARET VOORHIES HAGGIN TRUST ESTABLISHED IN MEMORY OF HER HUSBAND
JAMES BEN ALI HAGGIN

Preface

REPRESENTING some of Lafcadio Hearn's best work during his early newspaper career, the stories and sketches printed on the following pages portray a weird, brutal, yet colorful society—the levee life of Negro steamboat hands.

A Cincinnati reporter, Hearn wrote these pieces during 1874-1877. To get his material, he accompanied policemen on the beat, peered into levee haunts, witnessed the revels of roustabouts, and listened to their endless superstitions. The simplicity of their animal existence appealed to him, and he frankly admired their strength and beauty, their plaintive song and frenzied dance. Before he left Cincinnati in 1877, he had printed twelve narratives of levee life and lore in the *Cincinnati Enquirer* and *Cincinnati Commercial*. These he never reprinted himself. Six were subsequently published by Albert Mordell and Ichiro Nishizaki in posthumous miscellanies. The remaining six are reprinted here for the first time.

Excepting obvious errors of newspaper printers, I present the text of the stories and sketches without editorial alteration. I have, however, omitted subtitles, and in one instance I have altered a title. Hearn's titles and subtitles, together with other bibliographical data, are as follows: "A Child of the Levee," *Cincinnati Commercial*, June 27, 1876, p. 4, cols. 4-5; "Dolly / An Idyl of the

Levee," *Cincinnati Commercial,* August 27, 1876, 6:2-3, reprinted in *An American Miscellany* (1924), edited by Albert Mordell; "Banjo Jim's Story," *Cincinnati Commercial,* October 1, 1876, 1:5-6, reprinted in *An American Miscellany;* "Pariah People / Outcast Life by Night in the East End / The Underground Dens of Bucktown and the People Who Live in Them," *Cincinnati Commercial,* August 22, 1875, 3:1-3, reprinted in *Occidental Gleanings* (1925), edited by Albert Mordell; "Jot / The Haunt of the Obi-Man," *Cincinnati Commercial,* October 22, 1876, 2:2; "Ole Man Pickett / Something of His Ranches, and a Bit of His Biography / A Little of Life Among the Lowly," *Cincinnati Enquirer,* February 21, 1875, 1:3-4, reprinted in *Barbarous Barbers and Other Stories* (1939), edited by Ichiro Nishizaki; "Levee Life / Haunts and Pastimes of the Roustabouts / Their Original Songs and Peculiar Dances," *Cincinnati Commercial,* March 17, 1876, 2:1-4, reprinted in *An American Miscellany;* "Black Varieties / The Minstrels of the Row / Picturesque Scenes Without Scenery—Physiognomical Studies at Pickett's," *Cincinnati Commercial,* April 9, 1876, 4:6, reprinted in *Occidental Gleanings;* " 'Butler's' / Our Popular Ethiopian Restaurant / Its Bill of Fare and Its Guardian Owl," *Cincinnati Enquirer,* November 22, 1874, 1:3; " 'Mrs. Lucy Porter,' " *Cincinnati Commercial,* July 14, 1876, 8:2-3; "The Rising of the Waters," *Cincinnati Commercial,* January 18, 1877, 8:1; and "Genius Loci," *Cincinnati Commercial,* August 12, 1877, 6:4-5.

O. W. FROST

Contents

Preface	*page* v
Introduction	1
A Child of the Levee	9
Dolly	13
Banjo Jim's Story	23
Pariah People	32
Jot	49
Ole Man Pickett	54
Levee Life	61
Black Varieties	84
"Butler's"	91
Auntie Porter	95
The Rising of the Waters	99
Genius Loci	104

Introduction

CINCINNATI in 1869 was a city of manifest destiny. It was the largest inland city in the nation; it had a quarter of a million people and plenty of room to grow. Its expanding trade was fed by rivers, canals, and railroads. Cincinnati was clearly the railroad hub of the West. One editor modestly suggested that the lines east should really be counted as separate railways from the lines north and west, giving the city more railways even than New York.

Cincinnati was building with pride and care. The broad avenues, noble public buildings and monuments, and gracious suburbs would be needed as the city grew in greatness. The Longworths, the Thompsons, and the Tafts had built names and fortunes to be reckoned with. Cincinnati was a cultural oasis in the West and a publishing center for newspapers, magazines, books, and music. National political conventions returned again and again to this pivotal city in politics.

But Cincinnati was not a homogeneous city. Many of the names attached to the growing fortunes were German names. The Germans lived "over the Rhine"— north and east of the Miami canal, filling the space between the canal and the hills. The artisans and craftsmen, butchers and brewers lived a life of their own in their German city the size of Meissen or Göttingen today. They brewed their own beer, and made their own beergarden society and entertainment. They read their own newspapers, printed in German, and attended their German Lutheran churches. The architecture of these churches and of the German homes is still a dominant feature of Cincinnati. Along with the Germans there were nearly 20,000 Irish and a liberal sprinkling of French.

Less numerous than the Germans and Irish, but not less noticeable in the river area of the city were the Negro levee workers. The 1870 census showed 5,904 Negroes in Cincinnati; there were many more just across the river in Kentucky, and there were probably a large number not counted in the census. Near the river were many Negro establishments in the alleys and rows east of the public landing; the heart of Negro Cincinnati, however, was Bucktown, in the area of Sixth and Seventh streets east of Broadway. Bucktown overflowed into the open country to the east; there were shacks, small farms, and a few settlements or clusters of houses. The village of Springfield contained at least 600 Negroes. Two Negro Baptist churches, one African Methodist church, and three other Negro churches were listed in the 1869 Cincinnati guide. The same guide noted the existence of an orphan asylum for Negro children, though "no information is at hand concerning this institution." Considering the fact that the "equal rights" amendment was not ratified until 1870, it is interesting to note that in 1870 nearly one-sixth of Cincinnati's Negroes had attended school. There were in 1874 one Negro high and intermediate school and four Negro district schools employing eighteen teachers and officers.

Away from the riverfront area, many Negroes earned a living in domestic service, by farm labor, by tilling their own small plots of ground, by keeping store, by selling produce in the streets, a few by teaching or preaching.

However, in the riverfront area most frequented by Hearn the chief Negro occupations were hard labor as stevedores, dockworkers, porters, riverboat firemen or deckhands; boardinghouse or tavern operation; and vice, especially prostitution, gambling, and theft. Though it was not considered safe for strange white persons in the Negro section of the waterfront, particularly at night, and police protection was sometimes asked by white persons wishing to visit the area, it can be truthfully said that it was no safer for Negroes; anyone who looked prosperous was in danger. Often there were 50 riverboats along the levee at one time, their hundreds of deckhands and firemen "on the town" to crowd as much living, loving, fighting, drinking, and gambling into their hours ashore as possible. Cincinnati by 1870 had become notorious throughout the Midwest for its wide open waterfront. Violence was common, and arrests were numerous in spite of the fact that police generally did not intrude on the night life of the levee if they could help it. However, beneath the surface the levee was not always as rough as it seemed, as Hearn discovered quickly. There was a kind of cosmopolitan tolerance and acceptance that was the rule. Hearn noted particularly a lack of artificiality and pretense which served to emphasize the essential humanity common to all.

The levee people stayed on the levee and did not bother fashionable Fourth Street, the residential suburbs, or the concentration of Germans "over the Rhine." White Cincinnatians, both the prosperous few and the hardworking many, reciprocated by ignoring the levee. If a man made an exception some night, he was glad that the people of the levee neither asked names nor cared about them. The people of the more respectable, if not more prosperous, Negro settlements were also careful to let the white folks alone and not get in the way. They were ignored in turn: the most favorable kind of relationship they could hope at that time to achieve.

Just as in every other part of Negro America, Negro Cincinnati in 1870 represented the incomplete acculturation of a race of people brought largely from West Africa against their will from five to nine generations before. The acculturation process had paradoxically been both remarkably fast and remarkably slow. In some aspects of life the opportunity to imitate Western European civilization had brought the Negro practically into that civilization; in others, where the opportunity to imitate was denied by accident or design, the blend of African traditional materials and the Western European adaptations or accretions stamped the Negro as part of a clearly separate culture. Remnants of Africa were strongest in song, dance, superstition, charms and cures, proverbs, riddles and games. Hearn was to become a serious student of these aspects of Negro culture. The language of the Negro could be understood by listening white persons, particularly if they listened with care and had some experience with Negro speech; however, in all the dynamics of speech Negro America differed from white America. Pitch and intonation, word groupings and stress, idiom and even vocabulary varied so greatly from standard white speech that a white person could seldom understand Negroes talking to each other.

Hearn was much interested in the special characteristics of Negro speech, and he reported it in many of his newspaper sketches as carefully as he could, considering the limitations of the symbols he had to work with, which were quite incapable of duplicating the sound values of Negro diphthongs, glissandi, and junctures.

For these Negroes, morality operated on a different system from standard white middle-class morality. For one thing, they had had little chance for contact with middle-class whites. For another, they had had no training or need for training for social responsibility. A member of a slave community does not have to accept any type of long-range responsibility; his master is in control of his future and the future of his children. The more children he has, the more property for his master. Actually there was wide variation in the mores from one slave community to another: in one community a strong family loyalty and a considerable degree of responsibility would be encouraged, while in another a slaveowner found it to his personal advantage to foster a nearly complete family disorganization. Of course nearly all the adult Negroes in Cincinnati had migrated there from slave states before, during, and just after the war. Family disorganization among the Negroes in Cincinnati itself was influenced also by poverty and its accompanying submarginal housing which often crowded a dozen children and adults into a single inadequately heated and ventilated room.

Lafcadio Hearn came to Cincinnati at the age of nineteen. He had been sent there to shift for himself after an early life which left indelible marks on his character. Born on Leucadia, one of the Ionian Islands, son of a British army officer and his Greek wife, Hearn had come to Ireland at the age of two. Brought up there by a childless great-aunt, he was later sent to school in France and England, developing a personality, educational background, and social orientation that were to be at the same time his gravest handicaps and the motive force of his artistic achievement. He had been myopic from birth and to read had to place his nose practically on the page.

While still a boy he lost the sight of the left eye as a result of its being struck by an end of rope on the playground. After the accident he felt self-conscious about his appearance for the rest of his life, preferring to be photographed in profile or with downcast eyes. He was always ill at ease in company unless convinced that he was fully accepted. His psychological handicap was so great that it tends to obscure the purely physical handicap. He felt that spectacles were as much hindrance as help, and though he wore them when he first arrived in Cincinnati, he apparently discarded them soon after.

In 1869, then, Hearn was small and frail, overconscious of what seemed to him extreme physical deformity, insecure and even frightened in the presence of people. His speech seemed a bit strange to American ears. His tastes and ideas were no less strange; he liked the occult, the remote, the macabre. He searched the library and bookstores for Gothic novels, for Poe, Bulwer Lytton, Gautier, and Victor Hugo, and for accounts of cannibalism in the South Seas; he searched the city by day and night for new sounds, sights, and smells. Hearn at nineteen was not convinced (nor was he ever to be) that the God of Abraham exists or that he is to be obeyed. He was not convinced of the superiority of the white race or of the English-speaking peoples. He was not convinced that one's humanity grew greater as his wealth and station in life improved, or that things were necessarily right or wrong because most respectable people believed them to be. Traditions interested him greatly, but did not mold him. His view of the world was unique, not only for Cincinnati but for the nineteenth century.

Hearn combined an omnivorous interest in the world about him with a desire to record what he saw and felt.

His most successful subject in school had been English composition. Writing was one thing he could do well, and he knew it.

After several false starts and a transitional period of secretarial work, proofreading, and free-lance writing, Hearn became a reporter and feature writer for the Cincinnati *Enquirer* in 1872. He moved to the *Commercial* in 1875, and stayed with that paper until he left Cincinnati in 1877. His biographers have emphasized his poverty, his shyness, his quaint habits, his unusual choice of friends during this period. Actually he rather quickly proved that he was an extraordinarily fine reporter. He was versatile; he could handle with equal ease a review of the new foreign books, a murder story, or an imaginative feature supposedly written by a woman of the town. Sometimes he wrote in the impressionistic, rhapsodic style for which he was later to become famous; often in the Cincinnati days, however, his style approached the "perfectly transparent medium" of Defoe, as Hearn recorded what he saw, documenting segments of life and dialog in the Cincinnati of the seventies.

Of his features on life in Cincinnati, Hearn's Negro sketches stand out for several reasons. First, they are important human documents. They show by their insight and empathy that Hearn had great interest in and understanding of the Negroes he saw in the city. The sketches are perceptive and sympathetic, yet not highly subjective and romanticized. Ole Man Pickett deserves respect, Hearn shows, but he is no noble savage. Second, Hearn's sketches are just about the only picture we have of Negro life in a border city in the post-Civil-War period. They form an invaluable record of the customs, folkways, and family organization of the urban Negro; they form also a case study of the process of acculturation at a vital transitional point in American Negro history. Third, these sketches throw light on one of the most controversial parts of the Hearn biography. "What are you going to say about a white man who in the 1870's lived with a mulatto woman, whether he claimed to be married to her or not?" seems to be the dilemma of the biographer who encounters Hearn's relationship with Althea Foley. These sketches of Negro life, most of them written during the period of Hearn's life with Althea, contribute to the kind of understanding of Hearn that makes "saying something" or expressing moral judgments unnecessary.

Hearn was to go on in the directions which his Cincinnati sketches foreshadow. He was to live a cosmopolitan life in New Orleans, the West Indies, New York, and finally, for the last fourteen years of his life, Japan. He was to continue his study of other races—of the Negro in New Orleans and the West Indies, and of the Japanese. He was to continue his interest in folklore, and to collect songs, tales, and proverbs wherever he traveled. He was to publish some of the translations from the French he had made in Cincinnati, and to continue translating throughout his lifetime. He was to continue his versatile literary production, writing novels, sketches, lectures, and studies which were to achieve for him the fame some of his Cincinnati friends predicted (a few of them were to gain fame also—the artist Frank Duveneck and the writer on music and folklore Henry Krehbiel). Neither his fame nor his list of publications is complete; much Hearn material (mostly from the 1870's) remains undiscovered, and the full critical study of his many-faceted achievement remains to be written.

JOHN BALL

A Child of the Levee

SHORTLY BEFORE daybreak on Saturday morning a drunken negro was pulled out of the river at the foot of Broadway by two watchful patrolmen, who subsequently experienced considerable difficulty in bringing the man to the station-house, as he was actually insane from poisonous whisky, and struggled with maniacal fury. By the time he had been brought, dripping wet and muddy, to the office of the Hammond Street Police Station, the force of his mania had fairly expended itself, and he stood before the desk with an air of frightened bewilderment, like a sleepwalker suddenly aroused from his dangerous dreams.

"What's your name, Mr. Tired-of-Life," humorously asked the humorous Sergeant.

"My name," answered Tired-of-Life, in a voice husky with whisky and river water, "is Albert Jones."

"Albert Jones!" exclaimed the Sergeant, in a tone of serious surprise; "that man can imitate the whistle of any boat on the Ohio or Mississippi River. Give us the Wildwood or the Andy Baum, old fellow!"

The prisoner's face suddenly brightened; he drew himself up with something of a rough pride and exclaimed, in the tone of one long accustomed to interest a crowd, "Gentlemen, I will show you the difference between the whistle of the Wildwood and the Andy Baum. Listen to the Wildwood—coming in."

He suddenly threw up both hands, concave-fashion, to his mouth, expanded his deep chest, and poured out a long, profound, sonorous cry that vibrated through the room like the music of a steam-whistle. He started off with a deep nasal tone, but gradually modulated its depth and volume to an imitation of the steam-whistle, so astonishingly perfect that at its close every listener uttered an involuntary exclamation of surprise. Not only was the peculiar metallic bass of the steam-whistle imitated in all its sonorous profundity, but by some extraordinary use of his nostrils the negro also rendered the occasional sudden variations of the call from a lower to a higher key. Then he imitated the whistle of the Andy Baum, of the Bostona, Potomac, Charles Morgan, Mary Miller, Thompson Dean, Arkansas Belle, the old Robert E. Lee, and numerous deep-snorting towboats. The officers listened in silence and evident admiration, until at last the arrival of another prisoner broke up the entertainment, and the peripatetic calliope was hustled into a cell, where he long continued to awake familiar echoes of the Voices of the River.

The poor fellow has evidently a wonderful natural faculty of distinguishing and memorizing the many modulations of tone in the steamboat calls, and his power of

imitating them is something marvelous. All along the
Rows there indeed dwell many who know by heart the
whistle of every boat on the Ohio; dusky women, whose
ears have been trained by rough but strong affection, as
well as old stevedores who have lived by the shore from
infancy, and wonderingly watched in their slave childhood
the great white vessels panting on the river's breast. But
Albert Jones offers the typical exhibition of this peculiar
faculty. The steamboats seem to his rudely poetic fancy
vast sentient beings, as the bells of Notre Dame to the
imagination of Quasimodo, and their voices come to his
ear as mighty living cries, when they call to each other
across the purple gloom of the summer night—shouting
cheery welcomes in sweetly-deep thunder-tones, or shrieking long, wild warning. Other melody he seems to have
little conception of—neither the songs of the stevedore nor
the vibrant music of banjo-thrumming. The long echoes
of the steam calls and the signal whistles of the night patrolmen—sounds most familiar of all others, indeed, to
those who live on the levee-slope—form the only chords
of melody in his little musical world. Possibly to him the
Song of Steam is the sweetest of all musical sounds, only
as a great tone-record of roustabout memories—each boat
whistle, deep or shrill or mellow, recalling some past pleasure or pain in the history of a life spent along the broad
highway of brown water flowing to the Crescent City of
the South. Each prolonged tone awakes to fresh life some
little half-forgotten chapter in the simple history of this
Child of the Levee—some noisy but harmless night revel,
some broil, some old love story, some dark story of steamboat disaster, a vessel in flames, a swim for life. Probably
the first sound which startled his ears in babyhood was
the voice of a steamboat passing by his birth place; and

possibly the same voice may serve for his requiem some night when patrolmen do not happen to hear a sudden splash in the dark river. We left him slumbering in his wet and muddy rags, dreaming, perchance, fantastic dreams of a strange craft that never whistles, and is without name—a vessel gliding noiselessly by unfamiliar banks to a weird port where objects cast no shadows, and even dreams are dead.

Dolly

"THE LORD ONLY," once observed Officer Patsy Brazil,
"knows what Dolly's real name is."

Dolly was a brown, broad-shouldered girl of the levee,
with the lithe strength of a pantheress in her compactly-
knit figure, and owning one of those peculiar faces which
at once attract and puzzle by their very uniqueness—a face
that possessed a strange comeliness when viewed at certain
angles, especially half-profile, and that would have seemed
very soft and youthful but for the shadow of its heavy
black brows, perpetually knitted Medusa-wise, as though
by everlasting pain, above a pair of great, dark, keen,
steady eyes. It was a face, perhaps, rather Egyptian than
aught else; fresh with a youthful roundness, and sweetened
by a sensitive, passionate, pouting mouth.

Moreover, Dolly's odd deportment and peculiar attire were fancifully suggestive of those wanton Egyptian
women whose portraits were limned on mighty palace
walls by certain ancient and forgotten artists—some long-
limbed, gauze-clad girls who seem yet to move with a snak-

ish and fantastic grace; others, strong-limbed and deep-bosomed, raimented in a single, close-fitting robe, and wearing their ebon hair loosely flowing in a long thick mass. Dolly appeared to own the elfish grace of the former, together with the more mortal form of the latter. She must have made her own dresses, for no such dresses could have been purchased with love or with money, they were very antique and very graceful. Her favorite dress, a white robe, with a zig-zag border of purple running around the bottom, fitted her almost closely from shoulder to knee, following the sinuous outline of her firm figure, and strongly recalling certain pictures in the Egyptian Department of a famous German work upon the Costumes of Antiquity. Of course Dolly knew nothing of Antiquity or of Egypt—in fact she could neither read nor write; but she had an instinctive esthetic taste which surmounted those obstacles to good taste in dress which ignorance and fashion jointly create. Her prehistoric aspect was further heightened by her hair,—long, black, thick as a mane, and betraying by its tendency to frizzle the strong tinge of African blood in Dolly's veins. This she generally wore loose to the waist,—a mass so heavy and dense that a breeze could not wave it, and so deeply dark as to recall those irregular daubs of solid black paint whereby the painters of the pyramid-chambers represented the locks of weird court dames. Dolly was very careful of this strange hair; but she indulged, from time to time, in the savage luxury of greasing it with butter. Occasionally, too, she arranged it in a goblin sort of way, by combing it up perpendicularly, so that it flared above her head as though imbued with an electric life of its own. Perhaps she inherited the tendency to these practices from her African blood.

In fact, Dolly was very much of a little savage, despite the evidences of her natural esthetic taste in dress. The very voluptuousness and freedom of her movements had something savage about it, and she had a wild love for violent physical exercise. She could manage a pair of oars splendidly, and was so perfect a shot that knowing steamboatmen were continually fleecing newcomers by inducing them to bet heavily against Dolly's abilities in the Sausage Row shooting-gallery. Turning her back to the mark, with a looking-glass hung before her, Dolly could fire away all day, and never miss making the drum rattle. Then she could swim like a Tahitian, and before daybreak on sultry summer mornings often stole down to the river to strike out in the moon-silvered current. "Ain't you ashamed to be seen that way?" reproachfully inquired an astonished police officer, one morning, upon encountering Dolly coming up the levee, with a single wet garment clinging about her, and wringing out the water from her frizzly hair.

"Only the pretty moon saw me," replied Dolly, turning her dark eyes gratefully to the rich light.

Dolly was a much better character, on the whole, than her sisters of the levee, chiefly because she seldom quarreled, never committed theft, and seldom got tipsy. Smoke she did, incessantly; for tobacco is a necessity of life on the Row. It was an odd fact that she had no confidants, and never talked about herself. Her reticence, comparative sobriety, and immunity from arrest, together with the fact that she never lacked money enough for the necessities of life, occasioned a peculiar, unpleasant feeling toward her among the other women, which expressed itself in the common saying that Dolly was "putting on airs." Once it became suddenly fashionable on the Row to adorn

windows with pots containing some sort of blossoming
weed, which these dusky folks euphemistically termed
"flowers." Dolly at once "put on airs" by refusing to con-
form to the growing custom.

"Why don't you have any flower-pots in your window?" curiously queried Patsy Brazil.

"Because," said Dolly, "I ain't a-going to be so d—d
mean to the flowers. The Row ain't no place for flowers."

One of her greatest pleasures was to pet a little bandy-
legged negro child, whose parents nobody knew, and
whom old fat Maggie Sperlock had adopted. She would
spend whole hours amusing the little fellow, romping and
laughing with him, and twisting her extraordinary hair
into all sorts of fantastic horns and goblin devices in order
to amuse him. Then she taught him the names of all the
great white boats, and the names of the far cities they
sailed from, and the odd symbolism of the negro steamboat
slang. When a long vessel swept by, plowing up the yellow
current in curving furrows about her prow, and leaving
in her rear a long line of low-hanging nimbus-clouds, Dolly
would cry: "See, Tommy, how proud the old gal is to-day;
she's got a fine *ruffle* on. Look at her *switch*, Tommy; see
how the old gal's curling her hair out behind her." Dolly
could not read the names of the boats, but she knew by
heart their gleaming shapes, and the varying tones of their
wild, deep voices. So she taught the child to know them,
too, until to his infantile fancy they became, as it were,
great aquatic things, which slept only at the levee, and
moved upon the river through the white moonlight with
an awfully pulsating life of their own. She likewise made
out of a pine plank for Tommy, a funny little vessel, with
a cunning stern-wheel to it, which flung up the water
bravely as the child drew it along the shore with a cotton

string. And Dolly had no end of terrible stories to tell Tommy, about Voodoos—she called them "hoodoos"—people who gathered heads of snakes, and spiders, and hideous creeping things to make venomous charms with, by steeping them in whisky until the foul liquor became "green as grass." Tommy would have become frightened out of his little life at these tales, but that Dolly gave him a dried rabbit's foot in a bag to hang round his neck; for Dolly, like all the colored folks of the levee, believed a rabbit's foot to be a sure charm against all evil.

Of course Dolly had "her man"—a rather good-looking yellow roustabout known along the levee as Aleck. In the summer time, when the river was "lively," as the steamboatmen say, she was rather faithful to Aleck; but when the watery highway was all bound in ice, and there was no money on the Row, and Aleck was away on the Lower Mississippi or perhaps out of work, Dolly was decidedly immoral in her mode of life. But Aleck could scarcely expect her to be otherwise, for his money went almost as fast as it came. It was generally a feast or a famine with him. He did come home one spring with forty-odd dollars in his pocket—quite a fortune, he thought it, and a new silver watch for Dolly; but that was, perhaps, the great pecuniary event of his career. Somehow or other the watch did not keep perfect time, and poor Dolly, who knew far more about steamboats than she did about watches, opened the chronometer "to see what was the matter with it."

"Why, it's got a little hair wound around its guts," said Dolly; "of course it won't go right." Then she pulled out the mainspring. "Such a doggoned funny looking hair," further observed Dolly.

Unlike the other women of the levee, however, Dolly had a little respect for her own person, and did not sell her favors indiscriminately. On the contrary, she managed for a long time to maintain a certain comparative reputation for respectability. And when she did, at last, become utterly abandoned, perhaps the Great Father of each one of us, black and white, fully pardoned all her poor errors.

For it came to pass in this wise: Aleck, one summer evening, became viciously drunk at a Bucktown ball, and got into a free fight, wherein one roustabout, to use Dolly's somewhat hyperbolic expression, "was shot and cut all to pieces." Aleck was only charged at the Hammond Street Police Station with being drunk and disorderly, but inasmuch as it was not his first offense of the kind, he was sentenced to pay a fine of fifty dollars, and to be imprisoned in the Work-house for a period of thirty days. When the Black Maria had rolled away, and the gaping crowd of loafers had dispersed, after satisfying their unsympathetic curiosity, Dolly wandered into the City Park, and sitting down upon one of the little stone lions at the fountain, cried silently over the broken watch which Aleck had given her. She arose with the resolve to pay Aleck's fine as soon as the thirty days of his Work-house sentence had expired, and went slowly back to the Row.

Now when Dolly had fairly resolved upon doing a thing, it was generally done. We dare not say too much about how Dolly had resolved to earn that fifty dollars in thirty days—about the only way, indeed, that it was remotely possible for her to earn it on the Row. Those who know the social life of the Row will, however, understand the difficulties in Dolly's way. The sudden change in her habits, the recklessness of her life—compared with what it had been; the apparently absolute loss of all the little self-respect she once had, at once excited the surprise of

her companions and of the police officers, who watch closely every habitant of the levee. She bought food only when
she could not beg it, seldom paid for a cigar, and seemed
to become a ubiquitous character in all the worst haunts
of the Row, by night and day.

"If you keep on this way, Dolly," finally exclaimed
Patsy Brazil, "I'll 'vag' you." It was then nearly thirty
days since Aleck had been sentenced. Patsy, kindly but
always firm, never threatened in vain, and Dolly knew it.

It is hardly necessary to say, however, that Dolly had
not been able to earn the amount of Aleck's fine, nor is it
necessary to state how much she had earned, when Patrolman Brazil was obliged to threaten her with the Work-
house. She had one recourse left, however,—to sell her
dresses and her furniture, consisting of a stove, a bed, and
an ancient clock—for much less than their pitiful value.
She did sell them, and returned from the second-hand
store to her bare room, to fall into an exhausted sleep on
the floor, hungry and supperless, but happy in the pos-
session of enough money to pay "her man's fine." And
Aleck again found himself a free man.

He felt grateful enough to Dolly not to get drunk for
a week, which he naturally considered no small piece of
self-abnegation in return for his freedom. A keener-eyed
man in a blue uniform with brass buttons, who looked
into Dolly's great hollow eyes and sunken face with a
muttered "God help her!" better understood how dearly
that freedom had been purchased. Hunger and sleepless-
ness had sapped the vitality of Dolly's nervous though vigorous organization. At last Aleck got work on a Maysville
packet boat, and sailed away from the levee, and from the
ghost of what was once Dolly, waving a red, ragged hand-

kerchief from her window in defiance of Pickett's orders. Just before the regular starting time some one had "tolled" the boat's bell.

"Who's fooling with that bell," exclaimed Dolly, suddenly dropping her cigar. "It's bad luck to do that." She often thought of the bell again, when week after week the vessel regularly steamed up to the long wharfboat—without Aleck. Aleck had told her that he intended to "see God's people"—the roustabout term for visiting one's home; but she never thought he would have remained away from her so long.

At last one evening while sitting at Pickett's door, filing some little shirt-studs for Aleck out of a well-bleached beef bone, some one told her how Aleck had got married up at Maysville, and what "a tip-top weddin' " it was. Dolly said nothing, but picked up her beef bones and her little file and went up stairs.

"They never die round here," said Patsy Brazil, "until their will's gone. The will dies first." And Dolly's will was dead.

Some women of the levee picked her thin body up from the floor of the empty room and carried her to a bed. Then they sent for old Judge Fox, the gray-haired negro preacher, who keeps a barber-shop on Sausage Row. The old negro's notions of theology were probably peculiar to himself, yet he had comforted more than one dying woman. He closed his shop at once, and came to pray and sing for Dolly, but she heeded neither the prayers nor the strange slave-hymns that he sang. The evening gray deepened to night purple; the moon looked in through the open window at Dolly's thin face; the river reflected its shining ripple on the whitewashed walls with-

in, and through all the sound of the praying and singing
there boomed up from below the furious thrumming of
banjos and bass-viols, and the wild thunder of the dancers'
feet. Down stairs the musicians were playing the tune,
"Big Ball Up Town"; up stairs the women were chanting
to a weirdly sweet air, "My Jesus Arose."

> Oh, ain't I mighty glad my Jesus arose,
> Oh, ain't I mighty glad my Jesus arose,
> Oh, ain't I mighty glad my Jesus arose,
>   To send me up on high.

Here comes my pilgrim Jesus,
A-riding a milk-white horse;
He's rode him to the east and he's rode him to the west,
And to every other quarter of the world.
>   Oh, ain't I mighty glad, &c.

Here comes my master Jesus,
With heaven in his view,
He's goin' home to glory,
And bids this world adieu.
>   Oh, ain't I mighty glad, &c.

He'll blow out the sun and burn up the world,
And turn that moon to blood,
And sinners in——

"Hush," said Dolly, rising with a desperate effort.
"Ain't that the old gal talking?"

A sound deeper and sweeter and wilder than the
hymned melody or the half-savage music below, filled all
the moon lit levee—the steam-song of the Maysville packet
coming in.

"Help me up!" gasped Dolly—"it's the old gal blow-
ing off steam; it's Aleck; it's my man—my man!"

Then she sunk back suddenly, and lay very still—in the stillness of the Dreamless Sleep.

When they went to lay her out, they found something tightly clutched in one little bony hand—so tightly that it required no inconsiderable exertion to force the fingers open.

It was an old silver watch, with the main-spring pulled out.

Banjo Jim's Story

MELANCHOLY, indeed, is the river-view when a rainy day dawns in dull gray light upon the levee—the view of a rapid yellow river under an ashen sky; of distant hills looming dimly through pallid mist; of steamboat smoke hanging sluggishly over the sickly-hued current; and, drearier yet, the ancient fronts of weather-stained buildings on the Row, gloomy masses of discolored brick and stone with gaping joints and shattered windows. Yet of rainy nights the voice of wild merriment echoes loudest along the levee,—the shouts of the lithe dancers and the throbbing of bass viols and the thrumming of banjos and the shrieking of fiddles seem to redouble in volume.

On breezy, bright nights, when the stars glow overhead, and the ruffled breast of the river reflects the sky-purple or the rich silver of a full moon, the dusky folks seek mirth for mirth's sake. But in nights of foul weather and fog, some say the merriment of the Row is attributable to the same strange cause which prompts solitary men in desolate houses or desert places by night to seek relief from loneliness by waking echoes in the gloom with shout or song.

Ghostly at all times, especially to those who live in
old dwellings, are rainy nights; full of creeping sounds
and awesome echoes and unaccountable knockings and
mysterious noises, as of foot-falls upon ancient floors, that
groan when walked upon. Now, the old Row is faced with
old houses, and they say that of rainy nights the dead hide
in the shadowy old doorways and haunt the dark nooks
of the deserted dancing halls, which have been closed up
since the great flood. And the habitants of the levee fear
the dead with an unutterable fear.

"Look-a-hyar, ole gal," cried Banjo Jim to Mary Pearl,
when the poor woman was dying in her dance-house on
the Row,—"if you's a-gwine to die, don't you be a comin'
back hyar after you's done dead, cos' I'se a-gwine ober the
ribber—*I* is." And when Mary died, Jim went over the
river with several of the levee girls. For the dead may
not pass over the water, according to the faith of the
roustabout; and to the haunted the steamboat offers a
safe asylum from the haunters. But it is said that Mary
came back notwithstanding, and comes back ever and anon
on rainy nights, bringing with her the ghosts of many dead
friends—Winnie, the pretty-faced little white girl who died
at Pickett's dance-house; and Horse-headed Em, the tall,
wicked-eyed mulatto who drank herself to death; and Mat-
tie Phillips, the young quadroon who died at the Work-
house, folks say for want of morphine. There is a long,
deep basement under the building where Mary kept house,
with a great brick archway at the further end, behind
which is a dark bed-room.

It happened one night not long after the old dance-
house had changed hands, that a drunken levee girl wandered into that room to return, wholly sobered by terror,
with a weird tale of how she had seen by the flickering

light of a tallow-dip three dead women seated at a table—
Mary Pearl, and Jane Goodrich and Horse-headed Em,
and how Mary had "gobbled at her." Since then no one
dare sleep in that room alone. Maggie Sperlock, who lives
there, can also tell you about a little woman who comes
back sometimes to watch over her children—the waifs that
Maggie named and adopted, Sis and Tom and Howard.
Sis is never whipped, for Maggie says that whenever the
child is punished the dead mother will come in the night
to haunt the chastiser. Sis is a pretty brown child, with
big, dreamful eyes, and a strange habit of wandering in
solitary places, whispering to herself or to Somebody in-
visible to all others—perhaps the frail, fond, dark mother,
who came back silently in the night to protect her little
one. Maggie has become afraid of the child's elfish ways,
and vows that old Jot, the Obi-man, must have bewitched
her. But all attempts, kindly or unkindly, to make the
child speak of the viewless beings she held converse with,
or of the spectral fancies that seemed to haunt her little
brain, proved useless; the old foster-mother dared not
whip her for fear of the Shadowy Woman whom she had
seen one night bending over the sleeping child, as though
to bestow a ghostly kiss; and Sis was finally sent to a kind
relative in Bucktown, in the desperate hope of exorcising
her.

While Sis was whispering to herself in shadowy places,
and while that hideous story about dead Mary coming
back to "gobble" at lonely people in the dark, was being
discussed along the levee, folks began to remember that
there had been an extraordinary mortality in the Row
during the past twelve months. There was Dave Whitton,
the tall, thin violin-player of Pickett's dance-house; and
Uncle Dan. Booker, the withered old "piker," who used

to wander about the levee bent crescent-wise with age, and finally died in the Work-house, serving out a sentence of vagrancy; and pretty Winnie, the little dance-house cook; and Matt. Phillips, the morphine-eater; and Horse-headed Em; and the supple quadroon, Dancing Sis; and clumsy Jane Goodrich; and poor Mary Pearl, who died vainly trying to whisper some awful confession to Judge Fox— all had departed from the life of the Row in one brief year. Some said it must have been the great flood, which left its yellow slime and death dampness in the dance-houses, that had thus depopulated the Row. Some whispered that if one who could no longer cast a shadow in the moonlight had indeed returned to haunt the levee, other unwelcome people would surely follow to revisit their old friends and old resorts. Then folks began to talk about going over the river.

"Tain't no use a-sayin' dem tings am unpossible," gravely observed Judge Fox; "I b'lebes in de Bible, I does; an' I knows dar am folks roun' hyar a-talkin' to folks dat am done dead, an' a sinnin' awful sins agin de Lord." Perhaps the Judge was referring to old Jot.

At last, one stormy night—a night of black ragged clouds fleeing before the face of a gibbous moon—there came a spectral shock which paralyzed the Row with fright —Banjo Jim's story.

Since Pickett after the last inundation removed his establishment from No. 17 to his present location, the old dance-house has remained untenanted. By standing upon a chair or barrel one can obtain a good view of the interior through the narrow panes of dingy glass in the upper part of the door. It can then be perceived that the plaster has fallen away from the ceiling in great irregular patches; the bare walls still betray faintly verdant traces

of the last flood; the door of the wooden partition in the
rear lies unhinged upon the floor near a row of empty
barrels; spiders monstrous enough to serve for the dead-
liest of Jot's Voodoo decoctions have spun vast webs in
the dark corners; and a veil of pallid dust, thick enough
to muffle the echo of a heavy footstep, masks the planking
of the dance-room. Now, for some time previous to the
occurrence which we are about to relate, Matt. Adams
(who was born with a veil, they say), had been telling
people that strange noises shook the old dance-house on
rainy nights—the booming of a ghostly bass-viol, the heavy
sound of dancers' feet, and the echo of strange laughter,
"like the laughing of people long dead." "I listened at
the door one night," said Matt., "and I heard them talking; I heard Dancing Sis and Dave Whitton, and they
laughed in the dark, but I could not hear what they were
saying." After the girl told that story, Banjo Jim seldom
passed along the Row at night without a rabbit's foot in
the breast pocket of his woolen shirt.

Whether he forgot the rabbit's foot on a certain Fri-
day night, has not been recorded; but it is most likely that
he did, for he had managed to get very drunk at Maggie
Sperlock's, where the folks had been having a big dance.
It was nearly two in the morning when the ball broke up,
and Jim lingered last at the bar. When he went out, the
gloomy Row and the silent steamboats at the wharf, and
the great posts by the broken curb, seemed to reel about
fantastically to the music of the last set—"Big Ball up
Town." It was a hot, feverish night; the wild sky was
thronged with the oddest clouds, moving in phantasma-
gorial procession before a warm breeze that seemed to
blow from some volcanic land; and the horizon seemed to
pulsate with lightning flashes. Jim listened for a friendly

police whistle, the wanton laughter of a levee girl—even the footfall of a roustabout. But everything was silent as the silent boats; the voices of the levee were hushed; the windows were all dark.

"I b'leebe the Row am dead," muttered Jim. "I'll make de ole gal talk all de same." He seized his banjo, and staggered along the broken sidewalk toward Pickett's, thrumming furiously to the negro melody:

> "Ole Joe kickin' up ahind an' afore,
> An' a yaller gal a-kickin' up ahind ole Joe."

Suddenly he arrived at the broken steps opposite the deserted dance-house, tripped and fell headlong, his banjo clattering on the uneven pavement with a dying twang of musical reproach.

"Hell an' d—tion," observed Jim.

A burst of unearthly laughter followed the remark. Jim looked around him for the laughers, but saw nobody. He held his breath and listened. Sounds of negro merriment seemed to issue from the old dance-house—the "Kee-yah, kee-yah!" of roustabout laughter, the tramp of dancing feet, and the rapid melody of the "Arkansaw Traveler," furiously played upon a shrieking violin. Jim was too drunk to observe just where he was; the levee seemed to have grown a mile long, and probably he thought himself at the new ball-room. He staggered to the door, and found it fast; he rapped, and none responded. Then he rolled an ash-barrel, filled with garbage and cinders, under the window, climbed upon it, and peered in.

The old hall was filled with a pale, sea-green light—such an unsteady radiance as illumes the path of a diver in deep water—a light that seemed to ripple up from the floor, along the walls and against the shattered ceiling, though reflected by no visible flame. The room was filled with dancers, dancing wildly with goblin gestures, while upon the broken partition-door, placed across a row of empty barrels, stood the tall, thin figure of Dave Whitton, the dead violin player, furiously fiddling the "Arkansaw Traveler," his favorite air. And among the dancers Jim could recognize the familiar faces of many dead friends— Winnie and Dancing Sis, Em and Matt. Phillips, and all the dead girls of the Row, with withered Dan Booker sitting in a corner, sleeping over his basket as in the old days.

They laughed and seemed to speak to one another, but Jim could not understand what was being said, whether that they spoke in some unknown tongue or that the noise of the music drowned the voices of the throng. He observed also that the thick layer of dust upon the floor remained undisturbed by the feet of the eerie crew, and that the figures of the dancers cast no shadows. Dave Whitton's eyes flamed with an elfish light, and a faint streak of pale fire seemed to follow each stroke of the fiddle bow.

Jim thinks that he had been watching the dance for an hour when the scene commenced slowly to assume a new character. The weird figure of the phantom fiddler grew taller and weirder; his violin lengthened and broadened until its tones deepened into a hoarse roar, and the phosphoric light which followed his bow shone brighter. Simultaneously the figures of the ghostly dancers lengthened and commenced to tower toward the ceiling. Then the musician ceased to play the "Arkansaw Traveler;" the dance continued to the goblin air of "The Devil Among the Tailors." Jim began to fancy that the figures of the dancers were blurring and blending into one another, so rapidly did the phantoms elongate and twine about in the nightmare dance. He instinctively looked up at the musician to see whether he had grown to the roof. But that climax of ghastliness must have been reached while Jim was watching the nearest dancers. The long fiddler had not only grown to the ceiling, but was actually growing *along the ceiling* toward the window over the door, bending horribly over the crowd below. The terrified roustabout involuntarily reckoned that at this frightful rate of growth the specter's head would touch the window-pane in about sixty seconds. He began to wonder whether the goblin would then commence to lengthen downward, and coil about the ball-room like an anaconda. The rippling light on the wall brightened from pale green to a livid corpse-light, and Jim felt that matters were approaching a crisis. From the moment he had peeped through the window some hideous fascination held him there; he lacked even the power to scream. He felt he could free himself by one audible yell of terror, but he could not even whisper; some ghastly influence had deprived him of motion and voice. Suddenly his ear caught the silvery sound of a patrolman's whistle on Lawrence street—the police Lieutenant was making his early round, and the spell was broken.

"Gorramighty!" gasped Jim in horror, when a flood of light burst over the levee—a sheet of white fire, followed by an abysmal crash.

Five minutes afterward two police officers found an apparently dead negro lying in the rain, opposite the old dance-house, together with an overturned ash-barrel and a broken banjo.

"That flash struck right near here," said Officer Brazil. "It's Banjo Jim; wonder if he got struck?"

Officer Knox bent over, opened the roustabout's woolen shirt, and laid his hand over the man's heart.

"Guess he must have got struck," observed Knox, with a satisfied expression of countenance.

"By lightning?" queried Patsy Brazil, stooping to make an observation.

"Lightning whisky," said Officer Knox.

Jim says otherwise, and the levee folks no longer lounge about the battered doors of No. 17 during the night hours.

Pariah People

THE DISTRICT lying east of Broadway, between Sixth and Seventh streets, and extending to Culvert or thereabouts, constitutes now but a small portion of what was known some eight or ten years ago as Bucktown, and was once not less celebrated as a haunt of crime than the Five Points of the Metropolis. Lying in the great noisome hollow, then untraversed by a single fill, the congregation of dingy and dilapidated frames, hideous huts, and shapeless dwellings, often rotten with the moisture of a thousand petty inundations, or filthy with the dirt accumulated by vice-begotten laziness, and inhabited only by the poorest poor or the vilest of the vicious, impressed one with the fancy that Bucktown was striving, through conscious shame, to bury itself under the earth. To-day we find much of the horrible hollow filled up; and the ancient Bucktown is gradually but surely disappearing, not as though by reason of a *fiat* from the Board of Improvements, but as though the earth were devouring, swallowing, engulfing this little Gomorrah. And our modern Bucktown is thus, perhaps,

partly divested of its old terrors. Murders have become rare there, and vice tries to hide itself more successfully than of yore. There was a time when it sorely tried a policeman's soul to be ordered on a Bucktown beat, and when highway robbery and assassination were rather common occurrences in that locality. People can still remember how, in a certain low brothel there, masked by a bar, a negro levee hand blew a brother roustabout's brains all over the bar; and how the waiter girl related the occurrence with a smile to divers breathless policemen and reporters, at the same time wiping the blood and white brains off the counter with a cloth—like so much spilt beer. It was said in those days that many a stout man had been decoyed into a Bucktown den, and disappeared forever from public view; for there were scores of eerie-looking frames in the hollow, with a reputation scarcely inferior to that of certain lonely inns in the Hartz Mountains, which we used to read about in childish days with a feeling of nightmare horror. But now the policeman is su-

preme king in Bucktown; his will is law, his presence
terror, and every door opens promptly at his knock at any
hour of the night. The fugitive from justice hides there
still, but only with the certainty of being arrested; the
drunken stranger may be victimized by a panel game, but
if he squeals at once his lost property will generally be
forthcoming; and, in short, those who live in Bucktown
live under a reign of terror, and only because they can
find nowhere else to live—no other rest for the soles of
their sinful feet.

They are Pariahs, Sudras, outcasts—often outlawed
even from common criminal society for the violation of
laws held sacred by most criminals, and the outraging of
prejudices entertained and respected by the criminal or
non-criminal world at large. The inimity ordinarily con-
comitant with the admixture of race ceases to exist on the
confines of Bucktown; whites and blacks are forced into a
species of criminal fraternization; all are Ishmaels bound
together by fate, by habit, by instinct, and by the iron law
and never cooling hate of an outraged society. The har-
lot's bully, the pimp, the prostitute, the thief, the pro-
curess, the highway robber,—white, tawny, brown and
black—constitute the mass of the population. But there
are two other classes—very small indeed, yet still well
worth notice. The first is composed of those who have
lost caste by miscegenation; the second, that of levee hands,
who live in a state of concubinage with mistresses who remain faithful to them. Of the former class it is scarcely
necessary to say that white women wholly compose it—
women who have conceived strange attachments for black
laborers, and live with them as mistresses; also, women
who boast black pimps for their masters, and support them
by prostitution. Of the other class referred to, we may

observe that it constitutes but a part of the floating population of Bucktown, inasmuch as the levee hands and their
women are the most honest portion of this extraordinary
community. Consequently, they live there only because
their poverty, not their will, consents, and whenever opportunity offers, they will seek quarters up town, in some
alley building or tenement-house.

As the violation of nature's laws begets deformity and
hideousness, and as the inhabitants of Bucktown are popu-
larly supposed to be great violators of nature's laws, they
are vulgarly supposed to be all homely, if not positively
ugly or monstrously deformed. "A Bucktown hag," and
"an ugly old Bucktown wench," are expressions commonly
used in the narration by uninformed gossips of some Bucktown incident. This idea is, however, for the most part
fallacious. The really hideous and deformed portion of
the Bucktown population is confined to a few crippled or
worn-out, honest rag-pickers, and perhaps two or more
ancient harlots, superannuated in their degrading profes-
sion, and compelled at last to resort to the dumps for a
living. The majority of the darker colored women are
muscular, well-built people, who would have sold at high
prices in a Southern slave market before the war; the
lighter tinted are, in some instances, remarkably well
favored; and among the white girls one occasionally meets
with an attractive face, bearing traces of what must have
been uncommon beauty. Gigantic negresses, stronger than
men, whose immense stature and phenomenal muscularity
bear strong witness to the old slave custom of human stock
breeding; neatly built mulatto girls, with the supple, pan-
therish strength peculiar to half-breeds; slender octoroons,
willowy and graceful of figure, with a good claim to the
qualification pretty,—will all be found among the crowd

of cotton-turbaned and ebon-visaged throng, who talk alike and think alike and all live and look alike. To a philosophical or even fair-minded observer the vicious-ness and harlotry of this class are less shocking than the sins of Sixth street, or even than the fashionable vice of Broadway; when it is considered how many of the former have been begotten in vice, reared in vice, know of none but vicious associations, have never been taught the com-monest decencies of life, and are ignorant of the very rudiments of education.

Desiring to see the inner life of Bucktown the writer, some evenings since, accompanied a couple of police offi-cers in the search for a female thief, who had been shortly before observed fleeing to this city of refuge. Bucktown by day is little more than a collection of shaky and soot-begrimed frames, blackened old brick dwellings, window-less and tenantless wooden cottages, all gathered about the great, mouse-colored building where the congregation of Allen Temple once worshiped, but which has long since been unused, as its score of shattered windows attests. But by night this odd district has its picturesque points. Buck-town is nothing if not seen by gaslight. Then it presents a most striking effect of fantastic *chiar'oscuro;* its frames seem to own doresque façades—a mass of many-angled shadows in the background, relieved in front by long gleams of light on some obtruding post or porch or wood-en stairway; its doorways yawn in blackness, like entrances to some interminable labyrinth; the jagged outline of its dwellings against the sky seems the part of some mighty wreck; its tortuous ways are filled with long shadows of the weirdest goblin form. The houses with lighted win-dows appear to possess an animate individuality, a charac-ter, a sentient consciousness, a face; and to stare with pale-

yellow eyes and hungry door-mouth all agape at the lonely
passer-by, as though desiring to devour him. The silent
frames with nailed-up entrances, and roof jagged with
ruin, seem but long specters of dwelling-places, mockeries
in shadow of tenanted houses, ghosts, perhaps, of dwellings
long since sacrificed to Progress by the philosophical Board
of Improvements. The gurgling gutter-water seems blacker
than ink with the filth it is vainly attempting to carry
away; the air is foul with the breath of nameless narrow
alleys; and the more distant lights seem to own a phos-
phorescent glow suggesting foul marasmal exhalation and
ancient decay.

Following the guide down the sloping sidewalk of
broken brick pavement from Broadway on Sixth street
east, all along in the shadow figures in white or black are
visible, flitting to and fro in a half-ghostly way, or con-
gregated in motley groups at various doorways; and the
sounds of gossip and laughter are audible at a great dis-
tance, owing to the stillness of the night. The figures
vanish and the laughter ceases as the heavy tread of the
patrolmen approaches—even the tap of a police-club on
the pavement hushes the gossip and scatters the gossips.
These are the owls, the night hawks, the Sirens of Bucktown, the wayside phantoms of this Valley of the Shadow
of moral Death. They walk abroad at all hours of the
tepid summer night, disappearing from view by day into
their dens. Dens, indeed, is the only term which can with
propriety be applied to many of their dwellings, whereof
the roofs are level with the street, and the lower floors
are thirty feet under ground, like some of those hideous
haunts described in the Mysteries of Paris. For while some
old rookeries have been raised, others have been fairly
covered up by the fills of Culvert, Harrison, and lower

Sixth streets; houses that once stood on stilts and to which access was only obtained by ladders, are now under the roadway and can only be entered by crawling on hands and knees. Fancy a lonely policeman struggling with a muscular and desperate murderer, thirty or forty feet under ground, in a worse than Egyptian darkness! There are many reasons, however, why such noisome, darksome, miasmatic dens should be forthwith destroyed, or at least why leasing or renting them to tenants should be prohibited by law. It was found necessary, in Paris, some years since, to wall up certain dark arches under the ramparts, which had been used for dwelling places by the poorest of the poor; nearly all the children born there were deformed, hideous monsters.

"These," observed the patrolman, pointing with his club to the buildings between the corner drugstore and the first alley east of Broadway, "are occupied by people who claim to be respectable. They never give us trouble. East of this there is scarcely a dwelling that is not occupied by the worst kind of people." Nevertheless, this alley can not be said to mark the boundary between two classes, as it is lined with evil haunts. It is foul with slime, black with slime, and is haunted by odors peculiarly unsavory. Passing by its entrance, and subsequently by some three or four well known "ranches," as the patrolman terms them, we enter the house of Mary Williams, a mongrel building, half brick, half frame.

This place is notorious as a panel den, a hive of thieves, a resort for criminals and roughs of the lowest grade. The door is wide open, and the room within lighted by the rays of a lamp with a very smoky chimney. A bed with a dirty looking comfort, a battered bureau, a very dilapidated rocking chair with a hole in its bottom,

a rickety table, and a mirror, constitute all the furniture
of the apartment. The walls have not been whitewashed
or repaired for years; and the plaster has fallen away here
and there, in great leprous patches, baring the lath frame-
work beneath. Mary Williams and a black girl, with a
red bandana turban, receive the patrolman with a smile
and a nod of recognition. Mary is on her best behavior,
having escaped a long sentence but a week before through
the failure of a prosecuting witness to appear. A very
ordinary looking woman is Mary—bright mulatto, with
strongly Irish features, slight form, apparently thirty-five
years of age. This blood seems to predominate strongly
in the veins of half the mulattoes of Bucktown. The
dreamy Sphinx-face with well-molded pouting lips, and
large solemn eyes, and wide brows—the face that recalls
old Egyptian paintings, and is not without a charm of its
own—is never seen in Bucktown, although not an infre-
quent type of physiognomy in respectable colored circles.
The solemn, calm, intelligent thought, quiet will, dormant
strength of the Sphinx-face is never associated with vice.

Mary swore "to her just God" that no one was con-
cealed about the premises; but the policemen lighted their
candles and proceeded to examine every nook and corner
of the building, under beds and tables, behind doors, and
in shadowy places where giant spiders had spun gray webs
of appalling size and remarkable tenacity. The rear room
of the ground floor was a dark and shaky place—dark even
in daylight, being beneath the level of the alley. The
creaking of the boards under one's feet suggests unpleasant
fancies about the facile disposal of a body beneath. A
hundred robberies have taken place there. The fly once
fairly in the trap, the lights are blown out, and he is left
to make his exit as best he can, while the wily decoys,

"thridding tortuous ways," are soon beyond pursuit. Above is the equally notorious establishment of Jennett Stewart, now, indeed, partially robbed of its old terrors by the committal of some half a dozen of its old denizens to the Work-house. Here Officer Sissmann once narrowly escaped being murdered. There was a tremendous fight going on in the third story, and the patrolman had mounted the creaky staircase to the scene of action, when he was suddenly pounced upon by the belligerent crowd of harlots and ruffians. Out went the candles; the treacherous club split in twain at the first blow; and before he could draw his revolver Sissmann was thrown over the balusters of the top floor, to which he still managed to cling for life. While hanging there the women slashed at him in the dark with razors, and the men kicked at his clinging hands in the endeavor to force him to let go. But the officer's muscles were iron, and he held on bravely, though covered with blood from random razor-slashes, until his partner rushed up in time to turn the tide of warfare. The recollection of this incident conjured up some decidedly unpleasant sensations on the occasion of our visit, while wending our way up the steep ascent of black and rotting stairs, fitfully illumed by gleams from Patrolman Tighe's candle. A double rap with the hickory club on a plank door at the summit, causes its almost instantaneous opening, and shows a group within of three colored women and two men, the former clad only in night-wrapper and chemise, the latter in shirt and pants. A tall, good-looking mulatto girl, with long, black, wavy hair and handsome eyes, but who smokes a very bad stoga and squirts saliva between her teeth like an old tobacco-chewer, answers the patrolmen's queries:

"What are you doing here, Annie?"

"I was hiding."

"Who are you hiding from at 2 o'clock in the morning?"

"Chestine Clark, Mr. Martin; for Christ's sake don't tell him I'm here—he swears he'll kill me."

Chestine is something of a dandy ruffian in Bucktown —a tall and sinewy mulatto, who always resists officers when opportunity offers; and is altogether a very unpleasant customer. Clark's father is a respectable and well-to-do old man, and has helped his son out of several very ugly scrapes. Annie is "his girl," and the officer evidently puts faith in her statement, for he promises secrecy. Having looked under the beds and examined every corner, the patrolmen descend, to emerge by a door on the second floor out on the noisome alley in the rear. This alley used to be a frightful place of a summer night, being crowded with thieves and harlots like Sausage Row on a June evening. But Anne Russell, Belle Bailey and Rose Lawson having been sent to the penitentiary, for cutting or passing counterfeit money; while Ann Stickley, Annie Moore, Annie Fish, Jennie Scott, Matt. Adams, Addie Stone, Molly Brown, Annie Jordan, Gabriella Wilson, and a hundred other notorious females, have been shipped off to the Work-house. "I always made it a rule," said Sissmann, "to keep the greater part of those women in the Work-house during the time I ran that beat. Otherwise the life of a patrolman would not be worth a hill of blue beans there. Where the prostitutes collect the thieves always gather. There are now between one hundred and fifty and two hundred women from Bucktown in the Work-house."

There were two women in white dresses sitting on doorsteps a little further on down the alley—one a bright quadroon, with curly hair, twisted into ringlets, and a plump, childish face; the other a tall white girl, with black hair and eyes, and a surprisingly well cut profile. Both are notorious; the former as a Sausage Row belle; the latter as the mistress of a black loafer, whom she supports by selling herself. Her sister, once quite a pretty woman, leads a similar existence when not in the Work-house. The patrolmen point them out, and pass into a doorway on the south side of the alley, leading to the upper story of the dwelling tenanted by John Ham, bar-keeper. Mrs. Ham, an obese negress, with immensely thick shoulders, comes forward to meet the patrolmen.

"Who's up stairs, Mrs. Ham?"

"Dey's no one only Molly, fo' God."

"Where's Long Nell?"

"In de Wuk-hus."

"And little Dolly?"

"Wuk-hus."

"And crooked-back Jim?"

"Wuk-hus."

"Ah, they've cleaned out these ranches since I used to run this beat before. Come up, gentlemen." Through a dark hall-way, over a creaking floor to a back room, and the patrolman's club plays the devil's tattoo upon the rickety planks. The door is unlocked and "Molly" makes her appearance.

Molly is the colored belle of this district. What her real name is neither her companions nor the police officers know. So far she has never been in the Work-house. She seemed to be about eighteen years old, of lithe and slender figure; complexion a Gypsy brown; hair long and dark with a slight wave; brows perfectly arched and delicately penciled; dreamy, brown eyes; nose well cut; mouth admirably molded; features generally pleasing. But Molly is said to be a "decoy" and a thief, and her apparent innocence a sham. The room is searched and found empty.

"Where did you get these?" exclaimed Tighe, picking up from the table a handsome pair of jet bracelets with heavy silver setting.

"They were made a present to me."

"That's too thin! Who gave them to you?"

"A man up town."

"What man?"

[No answer.]

The officer lays down the trinkets with a frown; tells Molly that he has a good mind to lock her up "on suspicion;" and departs, looking unutterable things. "Did she steal them?" we ask.

"Oh, no," is the reply; "I only want to scare her a little, for I happen to know who gave them to her. It is a curious fact that business men and people of respectability get decoyed down here occasionally by girls like that, and get infatuated enough to bring them presents. She wouldn't tell, though, even if I locked her up."

Near here, a couple of doors away, is Joe Kite's place, concerning which horrid stories were once told; the old den kept by Addie Stone, a handsome but tigerish woman, now in the Work-house for cutting; and further on, the noisome underground den of Gilbert Page, who has lived in Bucktown for twenty-two years, and has paid over five thousand dollars for fines to the Clerk of the Police Court. Here fish and bad whisky and pigs'-feet are sold three stories under ground; and here a police officer was nearly murdered while trying to arrest a prisoner in the labyrinth

below. Over Joe Kite's lives a good-looking white girl,
with some outward appearance of refinement, and who
still retains that feminine charm soonest lost by a life of
dissipation—a sweet voice. This is Dolly West, or "Detroit
Dolly," as they call her, a colored man's woman, and one
of the princesses of Bucktown. "Indian Maria," a yellow-
skinned and hideous little woman from Michigan, with a
little red blood in her veins, lives with others in the building once occupied by Addie Stone. Last week Matt. Lee,
a mulatto girl, carved Indian Maria's ugly face with a
razor, and was sent to the Work-house therefor. And not
far from Culvert, in a two-story building known as Limber
Jim's, lives a very peculiar-looking woman, Belle Bailey,
just released from the Columbus Penitentiary. Belle is a
West Indian, tall and gracefully built, with a complexion
of ebony, but with beautiful hair, and features that are
more than ordinarily attractive in their aquiline strength.
Belle is not considered much of a thief, but she is danger-
ously quick with the knife. Indian Maria is not the only
Indian here. There is also Pocahontas, a tall, hawk-nosed,
yellow-skinned, superannuated sinner, who lives on Culvert street, back of the bar-room kept by the white des-
perado, Kirk, who has served a term in the Penitentiary.
Pocahontas claims to be related to John Smith, of Virginia—"you know all about John Smith, of Virginia."
Pocahontas, Indian Maria and a ghoulish-looking little
woman without any nose, who lives over Greer's grocery,
are all dump-pickers. So is Kate Miller, *alias* Hunnykut,
who lives next to Kirk's, on the Sixth street side. We must
not forget to mention Kate Hayes' den, the lowest thieves'
hole in Bucktown, which is situated next to Pocahontas',
and stands at the corner of Harrison and Culvert. Most
of these buildings are two or three stories under ground.

Culvert, between Sixth and Seventh, seems to mark the
boundary line, east and west, between ignorant poverty,
pure and simple, and ignorant vice of every description.
On Culvert the population is about half and half of either
sort; but from the fill up Seventh street north as far as
Pruden's Barracks—a tenement house—for harlots, or to
Mary Herron's den, still further up, wickedness reigns
supreme all through the hours of darkness. On the south
side of Seventh street matters are equally bad; and all
along the nameless alleys and the tumble-down rookeries
about the big factory in the heart of Bucktown, the sub-
limity of moral abomination abounds. The density of the
population here is proportionately greater than in any
other part of the city, although it is mostly a floating
population—floating between the work-house or the penitentiary, and the dens in the filthy hollow. Ten, twelve,
or even twenty inhabitants in one two-story underground
den is common enough. At night even the roofs are occupied by sleepers, the balconies are crowded, and the
dumps are frequently the scenes of wholesale debauchery
the most degrading. How it is that sickness is not more
common among this class, we confess ourselves unable to
comprehend. The black hollows are foul, noisome, miasmatic; full of damp corruption, and often under water,
or, better expressed, liquid filth. In the alley which runs
by the old Allen Church, on Fifth and Culvert, some
twenty feet below the fill, is a long, stagnant pool of exe-
crable stench, which has become a horrible nuisance, and
which never dries up. Insect life, the foulest and most
monstrous, lurks in the dark underground shanties near
by; and wriggling things, the most horrible, abound in
the mud without. There is here a large field for both the
Board of Health and the Board of Improvements to exer-

cise talent. At the corner of Culvert and Sixth is a hole
running into the sewer—a hole as deep as a well and as
wide as a church door, and only covered with a few broken
planks—splendid place to dispose of a body in. Then below the lots opposite Harrison and Culvert, where stands
the ruins of Gordon's oil factory and of Woods & Carna-
han's burnt out establishment, there is an immense well
uncovered save by some charred beams. Here Bucktown
thieves congregate in packs at times, and highway robberies, rapes, and brutal fights have been committed time
out of mind. That well should be filled up.

The search for the fugitive thief was continued by
the officers until the sky became a pale gray in the east—
down shaky ladders into cavernous underground dwellings, up rotten stair-cases into shaky frames, into hideous
dens hidden away between larger buildings looking out on
the alley. The sheepish humiliation of the debauchees,
when the light from the officer's bull's-eye fell upon them,
was sometimes pitiful. It was not uncommon to find white
men of respectable appearance, and well dressed, sleeping
in such dens. The police will seldom molest them while
they "behave themselves;" but the well known male thief,
be he white or black, is allowed no place in Bucktown to
hide his head, and if found in any den is at once kicked
into the street. The first instance of this which came under
our personal observation was in the brothel of a white
woman, known as "Fatty Maria," who keeps on Sixth,
near Culvert, opposite Kirk's. As a general rule no door
is at any time closed against the police; but on this particular occasion, the women evidently knew what was
coming, and all feigned slumber as long as they dared.
Finally, repeated rappings and terrible threats caused a
sudden opening of the door, and a fellow named Collison

was found by the officers sleeping between two women, and at once ordered to vacate the premises. He first feigned sleep and drunken insensibility to the "nippers," and a wholesome tapping with a club; finally, he refused to depart. The women took part, and Fatty Maria attacked one of the officers like a wild cat. He received her with a back-handed slap in the face that sounded like the crack of a whip, when she sprang to the mantle-piece and seized a razor. Before she could use it, however, she was disarmed by another patrolman, and held down, powerless, on a chair, while Collison was fairly flung out of the room and kicked into the exterior darkness. "If that woman did not harbor thieves," said the officer, "we could get along well enough with her, as she is generally quiet; but only this morning she pawned one of her beds and a bureau and a clock for $12, because she wanted to bail out a rascal from the Work-house."

During this episode at Fatty Maria's, a disgusting occurrence, which well illustrates the brutality of the Bucktown rough, occurred almost immediately across the way. There is a young white woman now in Bucktown, who spends the greater part of her existence in the Work-house for drunkenness, and whose degradation is such that she has even ceased to be known by name. On the day previous to our trip this wretched creature had been discharged from the Work-house, and returned to her old haunts. Some one had decoyed her into a low den, made her drunk and taken the most cowardly advantage of her condition, afterwards thrusting her into the street. Soon after some roughs half carried, half dragged her into Kirk's bar-room and poured some more poison down the poor creature's throat for similar purposes. When they heard the police approaching they dragged her out upon the sidewalk and propped her up in a sitting position upon some paving stones near the curb. Here she failed to attract attention while the officers passed down the other side, although in her drunken helplessness she fell sideways upon the stones, her hair streaming over the curb to mingle with the filth in the gutter. While the police were expelling Collison from Fatty Maria's a crowd of ruffians, white and black, lifted the unconscious woman, and carried her to a vacant lot in the hollow in rear of Kirk's, where they tore off part of her clothing. Before the police could reach the spot, the fellows fled beyond pursuit. The officers brought the wretched creature to a neighboring shanty, Kate Miller's. Kate agreed to take care of her, but expressed fears that the rowdies would return for their victim! It is comforting to think that in ten years hence Bucktown will have ceased to exist.

Jot

OCCASIONALLY, when the swarthy life of the Row becomes vitalized into unwonted activity by a fierce sun,
and swarms along the levee slope, as though imbued
with something of a lizard love for light and warmth, a
strange-looking being may be observed sauntering leisure-
ly through the many-colored crowd, gazing at all, speaking
to few, familiarizing with none. All make way for him;
noisy gossip ceases at his approach; the smiles of the Ser-
pent Women upon fascinated strangers suddenly vanish
as he passes by; he traverses the picturesque concourse
like an iceberg floating over a tropical sea, leaving a wake
of Arctic chill in the tepid water. He is tall and lean, but
his leanness bespeaks snaky litheness and subtle strength;
his long and bare feet seem to seize the projections in the
broken pavement with a sort of apish power. His complexion is a deep bronze—not the flushed, coppery bronze
of the brighter levee girls, but a dark, dull hue, like that
of old French statuettes. His head is bald, but his features
are framed with shaggy whiskers of iron-gray. The face is

Ethiopian, but peculiarly keen and intelligent; the eyes form its most remarkable feature—intensely brilliant, rapid, far-reaching—their brilliancy renders it very difficult to ascertain their color. This odd figure, straight as the jackstaff of a steamboat, and attired only in "full Mollies," woolen shirt and seven-gabled hat, is known and feared by the name of Jot. And the levee folk stand much more in awe of Jot than they do of the Almighty.

Jot is the Voodoo of the Levee—the necromancer and mystical high-priest of its fantastic superstitions—a prophet impotent to bless, but all-powerful to curse, ever silent in regard to his secret powers and dark knowledge—a solitary without friends or enemies, and a hater of women. What levee-girl ever dared to visit the wizard's den, save on "business?"—to seek a weird revenge or obtain unlawful counsel.

Until one has visited Jot's den, he can form no idea how far the fantasies of fable-makers regarding the habits and dwelling places of wicked wizards, may be realized even in the heart of a modern city. There were formerly two approaches to the obi-man's dwelling place, but one of them offering ingress from the Row, has of late been nailed up by Pickett, the leaseholder. Still through chinks in the barred doorway, a glimpse may sometimes be obtained of the old Voodoo, toiling by the light of a dim lamp. You must first pass through a long, low basement on the Row, divided into two apartments by a wooden partition, where resides a good-natured black woman, with the reputation of a fortune-teller, who is known as the "Funny Ole Gal." In the rear of this basement is a deep brick wall, with a small door in the left corner, opening on the strangest court imaginable—a narrow alley, about twenty-five feet long, blind at either end, and roofed seventy feet above the ground by a gigantic skylight of glass and iron. This "court" is but five feet wide, damp and foul; the high walls drip with noisome water, and windows open north and south upon it. It widens toward the summit, and on ledges far up above are suspended a number of sooty ladders, while in some of the southern windows, a few queer plants, growing in wooden boxes, turn their green leaves and blossoms outward and upward toward the dim light. A door in the north wall, opening immediately opposite that in the rear of the "Funny Ole Gal's" place, is the door which formerly opened into the home of the obi-man; and it is through chinks in this ancient entrance that he may be sometimes seen.

Jot's den is now approachable only from the Front street side, through the trap doors of a deep cellar, and down a flight of pine plank steps, made by Jot himself. On descending the pine steps you are stopped by a strong wooden partition and stout door, also the work of Jot's hands. Beyond is a corridor of more than Egyptian darkness, sloping downward into the den itself.

When the eyes become a little accustomed to the gloom, the visitor finds himself in a small underground apartment, flanked by the foundations of the building above, and wholly without flooring. The earth is soft and damp under the feet; the black-beamed roof is festooned with enormous cobwebs above; a wood-fire glows through the cracked sides of a ruined monkey-stove in one corner; and upon a rude pine table burns a lamp with five tongues of pointed flame, fed by the gas of a volatile oil—the separate flames being of such different lengths and so curved as to convey the idea of upward clutching fingers of fire.

A stench of indescribable foulness creeps into the den from the narrow court in the rear. Here Jot works, cooks, washes, sleeps and receives mysterious visits.

"Why don't you sweep away those awful cobwebs?" we asked Jot.

"Well, I don't let them spin webs over my bed," answered the Voodoo, with a somewhat sinister laugh; "but I don't want to prevent them doing as they please any where else."

He held up the gasoline lamp to the sooty beams overhead, and invited us to behold such forests of webs and huge colonies of many-legged life as would terrify even an entomologist. There were tribes of ghostly spiders with tiny bodies and infinitely extended legs, who spun flimsy webs of pale gray; there were hosts of black, powerful arachnidae, fat-bellied and venomous, who manufactured strong, greasy webs of disgusting tenacity; there were speckled spiders of surprising size, and pale multitudes of swarming young. They could have been swept down by the basinful. Here and there we noticed masses of tangled web which bore the appearance of having been placed in position by human hands, after having been detached from elsewhere. Certainly there appeared to be every foundation for the popular belief in regard to Jot's culture of poisonous spiders; and what filthy reptile life he might secretly nourish in the moist clay under his feet— what frightful decoctions might be prepared in the rusty iron kettle simmering upon the stove, we dared not even imagine.

Hither, it is whispered, come stealthily at intervals visitors seeking revenge for a wrong, vengeance upon a rival, love-spells for the revival of a dead passion or the maintenance of a new affection, charms against dangers by fire and flood, and talismans to repel the silent steps of dead men from the threshold.

But perhaps Jot is, after all, only an intelligent hermit, quick to take advantage of the superstitious fancies inspired by his eccentricities, preferring a damp cellar to live in because his rent is only fifty cents a week; despising the reckless life of the Row, through superior moral intuition; and suffering spiders to propagate in his dwelling rather than undertake the disagreeable task of killing them.

Ole Man Pickett

WHEN AN EXHAUSTIVE history of the Queen City comes
to be written, among the names of those who labored both
for her weal and woe, few will be more conspicuous than
that of Henry Pickett, now the hero and chief proprietor
of that fashionable boulevard known as Sausage Row.
Who has not heard of "ole man" Pickett and his ranches,
but who knows what he has done for and against Cincinnati? Who has not often seen Sausage Row in print, but
who knows where it is located, and how many human
hives exist along its border? Who has not seen a record
of some criminal, or of some stolen property being found
in Pickett's ranch, but who knows what these ranches are,
and what they contain? We paid Pickett and his posses-
sions a visit the other evening, when some seventy-five or
a hundred of the dusky frequenters of his ranches were
reveling in waltzes, polkas, lances and quadrilles. We had
ample opportunity to view the premises, and plenty of
ears to hear the "ole man's" story, though the rattling of
tinware, the strains from a cracked violin, a dismal guitar

and a wheezy bass viol, together with the jingling of
glasses, and the calls of "Swing partners, forward and back,
first fo' right and left," were fairly deafening to us. The
premises consist of three or four saloons, eating and dance-
rooms, over which Pickett has a personal supervision. The
two or three other "cribs" or places in the row Pickett
partially controls, he being a sub-leaser. The particular
ranch which we visited on the evening in question, like
all the others, is in a basement, and except on one side is
entirely underground. The bar is in the front room, and
the dancing place is located immediately in the rear. The
bar-room receives a little of the light of day, but the dance-
room, save when lit by the faint flickerings of a coal-oil
lamp, is in perpetual darkness. Rafters and boards answer the purpose of ceiling, and whitewashed stone walls
are the linings on every side. In the extreme rear end of
the dance-room the proprietor has had partitioned off a
small bed-room where he sleeps, his sleeping companion
being his only son, a wooly-head of some ten summers, and
a half-dozen homeless curs which, out of pity, he has res-
cued from the street. The bar, dance and bed-rooms altogether do not cover more than sixty-five by twenty feet,
and yet in this small space the host manages daily, and
nightly too, to entertain from seventy to a hundred Ameri-
canized Ethiopians. A dark skin is a necessary passport
into Pickett's places. "White trash" revelers, with one or
two rare exceptions, are never admitted. A poor, half
idiotic white girl may be seen in here occasionally, but she
has been specially privileged because she has a negro for
her "feller." In their dances very little order and a great
deal of whisky prevails, and yet from these dances very
few disturbances have been known to arise. The average
white man, inspired by the same kind of lightning which

these black and thirsty warriors imbibe, would only find
vent for his exuberance in playfully firing a few random
shots from a well loaded revolver, or in frisking around
promiscuously with an illy proportioned bowie-knife. A
mixture of brimstone, prussic acid, snake fangs and other
harmless ingredients, makes the white man unpleasantly
demonstrative; but down on Sausage Row it seems to
make the black man submissive and even good natured.
No matter how drunk Pickett's guests become, over them
he has very rarely lost his seemingly magnetic influence.
The admission of white scum to his quarters, he appre-
hends, would break the spell, and so he keeps it out. He
says his receptions now move off pleasantly, and so long
as the colored man is his only patron he expects they will
continue to do so.

As we entered the other evening and looked upon
the three musicians sawing and picking away, the leader
yelling off the changes in a low guttural tone, twenty or
thirty dancers on the floor shuffling around amid rivulets
of tobacco-seasoned saliva, sixty or seventy dusky faces
looking on, low-crowned hats ornamenting the heads of
males, and streaming, gorgon-like looking hair the heads
of females, a pale, sickly light from the lamp shed over
the scene, the sensation became weird in the extreme.

The closing of navigation on the Ohio has had a material effect on Pickett's net receipts, inasmuch as the most
of his patrons are river men. The stoppage of work is
usually a signal for these river rats to ask for credit, as
they very rarely husband any thing. Pickett never turns
any man away from him hungry. If asked for credit he
almost uniformly gives it, and then trusts to luck and his
customer's honesty for pay. During the past few weeks of
cold weather this old man, who has been considered as

utterly destitute of any of the milk of human kindness, has been feeding and warming nearly a hundred destitute negroes, whom, were it not for him, the city would be obliged to support. He has fed and warmed them, too, when very little money was realized for the same. He charges them twenty-five cents for a regular "white folks' meal at a table," ten cents for a lunch, and ten cents for the privilege of sleeping by his fire. He adheres to a European plan with a reasonable schedule of prices. His charges, when not cashed, are entered upon a book, which the bar-tender keeps; as Pickett himself is unable either to read or even to sign his own name. Henry Pickett is now over sixty-four years of age, and was born a slave in Goochland County, Virginia. George Pickett, an owner of over five hundred slaves, was his father, and a member of the Virginia Legislature. His mother, an ebony black woman, was owned by a heavy planter and slave-owner named Charles Hawchins. Hawchins had hired out some of his chattels to George Pickett, Henry's mother among them, and that's the way Henry came about. Hawchins dying, Henry fell into the hands of his heirs, under the care of an ugly overseer. This was very galling to him, and so he took a French leave of his friends and made for the woods. He was hunted down by bloodhounds, captured, placed in irons, lashed with raw-hides, rubbed down with salt and water and then set to work again. He had grown to be a perfect Titan in size, nerve and strength, and had come to think that slavery was not his proper element, and so he ran away again. This time he lived for over a year in the woods, feeding upon such fruit as he could find and such food as neighboring slaves would bring him. With this kind of life he became tired, and so voluntarily gave himself up to his old masters; soon had a fight with the overseer; was badly cut up, marks of which he now bears; became a cheap "nigger" in consequence, and was sold. A Richmond man named James Benworth was the purchaser. Benworth had an eye to business, and immediately offered Pickett the privilege of buying himself for a thousand dollars' consideration. This was to be a legitimate freedom, and Pickett jumped at the offer. He immediately resumed the responsibility of porter at the old Exchange Hotel, Richmond, and began the laborious task of buying his freedom. He had accumulated nine hundred dollars, and paid over to his master, when the original offer was reconsidered, and he was again on the block. This time he was sold to a Mr. Thornton, and placed as a steward on a James River packet-boat, with an understanding that if he valued his liberty $1,800 worth he could have it by paying for it. Thornton was as good as his word, finally received his $1,800, and Pickett, at the age of forty, was his own master for the first time. He continued with the packet company until he had accumulated $800 more and paid over for his wife and child, when, in 1854, he came to Cincinnati. For the first few years of his life in this city he lived and worked for a sporting man on Baker street, known as Tom Curran. Having accumulated considerable, he bought a farm, sawmill and grocery near Xenia, Greene County, where, for a time, he was prosperous, but where, after three years, he was, to use his own language, "busted up." He says he lost four or five thousand dollars in this speculation. He then came back to this city and opened a coffee-house in a cellar on Fourth street, between Main and Sycamore. The Rev. Dr. Weeds was his landlord. "Very accommodating man dat Doctor was," said Pickett; "let me sell any thing I wanted to in his ole cella." The coffee-house

on Fourth street, however, did not pan out well, and so
another move was made; this time to a low, dingy, dark
hole on Sixth street, where he, for the first time, became
notorious. His place ranked among the lowest sinks in
Cincinnati. He made lots of money here, however, but
being again and again hauled up by the police, his money
melted away in a most mysterious manner. Again and
again would he be accused of this and that crime, but
through his innocence, or mayhap his lucre, he would invariably escape. Sixth street finally became too warm, too
aristocratic or too something, and so he again migrated,
making his final stand on Sausage Row, just east of the
old Spencer House. In this place his fortune, like his
whole life, has been very checkered. Here he has lost wife
and children, and here he has cleared and sunk thousands
of dollars. Here he has acquired the reputation of being
alike the respecter of the light fingers of the prig and the
strong arm of the law. Here policemen, searching for
missing property, come for information, and here thieves
searching for customers find a market. In the aid lent to
the discovery of crime the weal of the city is here fostered,
but in the encouragement given to the criminal her woe is
also furthered. In the feeding and trusting of scores of
colored vagrants which hang about his ranch he keeps
them from the Work-house, and so contributes to the city's
good by saving her a heavy expense. His colored brethren
have always found him an ugly enemy and a reliable
friend. The descendants of Ham, from the junction of the
Allegheny to the Mississippi, know him, respect him, and
fear him. Not a policeman in Cincinnati who has ever
had any thing to do with Pickett will not have a good word
to say for him, though at the same time they paradoxically
claim him to be a bad man. Cincinnati lawyers, who have

again and again helped him out of and away from some
very ugly snags in the Police Court, know that he is generally prompt at paying their fees. City missionaries have
found him serious, and city offenders have found him gay.
Among Romans he always does as the Romans do. He is
crafty and curious and frank. He is an interesting phe-
nomenon over which the phrenological disciples of Fowler
would puzzle. Like a certain other personage occasionally
heard of, when sick Pickett a saint would be, but when
well a Pickett of a saint is he. He is now laid up with
what he calls "busted veins," his lower limbs being con-
stantly swollen, and he is therefore ready to converse upon
death, hell, judgment, and other cheerful subjects. As an
old man he can see that his days of probation are rapidly
tallying. He wants to dispose of his business, but can find
no purchaser. He says he wants to go to the home of his
only daughter, now in Richmond, Virginia, and there die.
With the expected "blues" of sickness he thinks his friends
are deserting him. He fears an attack of the "King of Terrors" in Cincinnati, but believes he could meet him man-
fully in Richmond. In Cincinnati he believes he has been
too often pushed to the wall, that in adversity all men
would forsake him, and that in death he might exclaim
like Logan of old, "Who is there to mourn for"—Pickett.

Levee Life

ALONG THE RIVER-BANKS on either side of the levee slope, where the brown water year after year climbs up to the ruined sidewalks, and pours into the warehouse cellars, and paints their grimy walls with streaks of water-weed green, may be studied a most curious and interesting phase of life—the life of a community within a community,—a society of wanderers who have haunts but not homes, and who are only connected with the static society surrounding them by the common bond of State and municipal law. It is a very primitive kind of life; its lights and shadows are alike characterized by a half savage simplicity; its happiness or misery is almost purely animal; its pleasures are wholly of the hour, neither enhanced nor lessened by anticipation of the morrow. It is always pitiful rather than shocking; and it is not without some little charm of its own—the charm of a thoughtless existence, whose virtues are all original, and whose vices are for the most part foreign to it. A great portion of this levee-life haunts also the subterranean hovels and ancient frame buildings of the district lying east of Broadway to Culvert street, between Sixth and Seventh streets. But, on a cool spring evening, when the levee is bathed in moonlight, and the torch-basket lights dance redly upon the water, and the clear air vibrates to the sonorous music of the deep-toned steam-whistle, and the sound of wild banjo-thrumming floats out through the open doors of the levee dance-houses, then it is perhaps that one can best observe the peculiarities of this grotesquely-picturesque roustabout life.

Probably less than one-third of the stevedores and 'longshoremen employed in our river traffic are white; but the calling now really belongs by right to the negroes, who are by far the best roustabouts and are unrivaled as firemen. The white stevedores are generally tramps, willing to work only through fear of the Work-house; or, some times laborers unable to obtain other employment, and glad to earn money for the time being at any employment. On board the boats, the whites and blacks mess separately and work under different mates, there being on an average about twenty-five roustabouts to every boat which unloads at the Cincinnati levee. Cotton boats running on the Lower Mississippi, will often carry sixty or seventy deck hands, who can some seasons earn from forty-five dollars to sixty dollars per month. On the Ohio boats the average wages paid to roustabouts will not exceed $30 per month.

'Longshoremen earn fifteen and twenty cents per hour, according to the season. These are frequently hired by Irish contractors, who undertake to unload a boat at so much per package; but the first-class boats generally contract with the 'longshoremen directly through the mate, and sometimes pay twenty-five cents per hour for such labor. "Before Freedom," as the colored folks say, white laborers performed most of the roustabout labor on the steamboats; the negroes are now gradually monopolizing the calling, chiefly by reason of their peculiar fitness for it. Generally speaking, they are the best porters in the world; and in the cotton States, it is not uncommon, we are told, to see negro levee hands for a wager, carry five-hundred-pound cotton-bales on their backs to the wharfboat. River men, to-day, are recognizing the superior value of negro labor in steamboat traffic, and the colored roustabouts are now better treated, probably, than they have been since the war. Under the present laws, too, they are better protected. It used at one time to be a common thing for some ruffianly mate to ship sixty or seventy stevedores, and, after the boat had taken in all her freight, to hand the poor fellows their money and land them at some small town, or even in the woods, hundreds of miles from their home. This can be done no longer with legal impunity.

Roustabout life in the truest sense is, then, the life of the colored population of the Rows, and, partly, of Bucktown—blacks and mulattoes from all parts of the States, but chiefly from Kentucky and Eastern Virginia, where most of them appear to have toiled on the plantations before Freedom; and echoes of the old plantation life still live in their songs and their pastimes. You may hear old Kentucky slave songs chanted nightly on the

steamboats, in that wild, half-melancholy key peculiar to
the natural music of the African race; and you may see
the old slave dances nightly performed to the air of some
ancient Virginia-reel in the dance-houses of Sausage Row,
or the "ball-rooms" of Bucktown. There is an intense
uniqueness about all this pariah existence; its boundaries
are most definitely fixed; its enjoyments are wholly sensual,
and many of them are marked by peculiarities of a strictly
local character. Many of their songs, which have never
appeared in print, treat of levee life in Cincinnati, of all
the popular steamboats running on the "Muddy Water,"
and of the favorite roustabout haunts on the river bank
and in Bucktown. To collect these curious songs, or even
all the most popular of them, would be a labor of months,
and even then a difficult one, for the colored roustabouts
are in the highest degree suspicious of a man who approaches them with a note-book and pencil. Occasionally,
however, one can induce an intelligent steamboatman to
sing a few river songs by an innocent bribe in the shape
of a cigar or a drink, and this we attempted to do with
considerable success during a few spare evenings last week,
first, in a popular roustabout haunt on Broadway, near
Sixth, and afterward in a dingy frame cottage near the
corner of Sixth and Culvert streets. Unfortunately some
of the most curious of these songs are not of a character
to admit of publication in the columns of a daily newspaper; but others which we can present to our readers
may prove interesting. Of these the following song, "Number Ninety-Nine," was at one time immensely popular
with the steamboatmen. The original resort referred to
was situated on Sixth and Culvert street, where Kirk's
building now stands. We present the song with some necessary emendations:

"You may talk about yer railroads,
    Yer steamboats and can-*el*
If 't hadn't been for Liza Jane
    There wouldn't a bin no hell.
    Chorus—Oh, ain't I gone, gone, gone,
        Oh, ain't I gone, gone, gone,
        Oh, ain't I gone, gone, gone,
        Way down de ribber road.

"Whar do you get yer whisky?
    Whar do you get yer rum?
I got it down in Bucktown,
    At Number Ninety-nine.
    Chorus—Oh, ain't I gone, gone, gone, &c.

"I went down to Bucktown,
    Nebber was dar before,
Great big niggah knocked me down,
    But Katy barred the door.
    Chorus—Oh, ain't I gone, gone, gone, &c.

"She hugged me, she kissed me,
    She tole me not to cry;
She said I was de sweetest thing
    Dat ebber libbed or died.
    Chorus—Oh, ain't I gone, gone, gone, &c.

*   *   *   *   *   *   *   *

"Yonder goes the Wildwood.
    She's loaded to the guards,
But yonder comes the Fleetwood,
    An' she's the boat for me.
    Chorus—Oh, ain't I gone, gone, gone, &c."

The words, " 'Way down to Rockingham," are sometimes substituted in the chorus, for " 'way down de ribber
road."

One of the most popular roustabout songs now sung
on the Ohio is the following. The air is low, and melan-

choly, and when sung in unison by the colored crew of a
vessel leaving or approaching port, has a strange, sad
sweetness about it which is very pleasing. The two-fold
character of poor Molly, at once good and bad, is somewhat typical of the stevedore's sweetheart:

> Molly was a good gal and a bad gal, too.
> > Oh Molly, row, gal.
> Molly was a good gal and a bad gal, too.
> > Oh Molly, row, gal.

> I'll row dis boat and I'll row no more,
> > Row, Molly, row, gal.
> I'll row dis boat, and I'll go on shore,
> > Row, Molly, row, gal.

> Captain on the biler deck a-heaving of the lead,
> > Oh Molly, row, gal.
> Calling to the pilot to give her, "Turn ahead,"
> > Row, Molly, row, gal.

Here is another to a slow and sweet air. The chorus,
when well sung, is extremely pretty:

> > Shawneetown is burnin' down,
> > > Who tole you so?
> > Shawneetown is burnin' down,
> > > Who tole you so?

> Cythie, my darlin' gal,
> > Who tole you so?
> Cythie, my darlin' gal,
> > How do you know?
> Chorus—Shawneetown is burnin', &c.

> How the h—l d'ye 'spect me to hold her,
> > Way down below?
> I've got no skin on either shoulder,
> > Who tole you so?
> Chorus—Shawneetown is burnin', &c.

De houses dey is all on fire,
 Way down below.
De houses dey is all on fire,
 Who tole you so?
Chorus—Shawneetown is burnin', &c.

My old missus tole me so,
 Way down below.
An' I b'lieve what ole missus says,
 Way down below.
Chorus—Shawneetown is burnin', &c.

The most melancholy of all these plaintive airs is that to which the song "Let her go by" is commonly sung. It is generally sung on leaving port, and sometimes with an affecting pathos inspired of the hour, while the sweethearts of the singers watch the vessel gliding down stream.

I'm going away to New Orleans!
 Good-bye, my lover, good-bye!
I'm going away to New Orleans!
 Good-bye, my lover, good-bye!
  Oh, let her go by!

She's on her way to New Orleans!
 Good-bye, my lover, good-bye!
She bound to pass the Robert E. Lee,
 Good-bye, my lover, good-bye!
  Oh, let her go by!

I'll make dis trip and I'll make no more!
 Good-bye, my lover, good-bye!
I'll roll dese barrels, I'll roll no more!
 Good-bye, my lover, good-bye!
  Oh, let her go by!

An' if you are not true to me,
 Farewell, my lover, farewell!
An' if you are not true to me,
 Farewell, my lover, farewell!
  Oh, let her go by!

The next we give is of a somewhat livelier description. It has, we believe, been printed in a somewhat different form in certain song books. We give it as it was sung to us in a Broadway saloon:

> I come down the mountain,
>   An' she come down the lane,
> An' all that I could say to her
>   Was, "Good bye, 'Liza Jane."
>
> Chorus—Farewell, 'Liza Jane!
>   Farewell, 'Liza Jane!
>   Don't throw yourself away, for I
>   Am coming back again.
>
> I got up on a house-top,
>   An' give my horn a blow;
> Thought I heerd Miss Dinah say,
>   "Yonder comes your beau."
>   [Chorus.]
>
> Ef I'd a few more boards,
>   To build my chimney higher,
> I'd keep aroun' the country gals,
>   Chunkin' up the fire.
>   [Chorus.]

The following are fragments of rather lengthy chants, the words being almost similar in both, but the choruses and airs being very different. The air of the first is sonorous and regularly slow, like a sailor's chant when heaving anchor; the air of the next is quick and lively.

> "Belle-a-Lee's got no time,
>   Oh, Belle! oh, Belle!
> Robert E. Lee's got railroad time,
>   Oh, Belle! oh, Belle!

> "Wish I was in Mobile Bay,
>   Oh, Belle! oh, Belle!
> Rollin' cotton by de day,
>   Oh, Belle! oh, Belle!

*   *   *   *   *   *   *   *

> "I wish I was in Mobile Bay,
>   Rollin' cotton by de day,
>   Stow'n' sugar in de hull below,
>   Below, belo-ow,
>   Stow'n' sugar in de hull below!

"De Natchez is a new boat; she's just in her prime,
Beats any oder boat on de New Orleans line.
         Stow'n' sugar in de hull below, &c.

"Engineer, t'rough de trumpet, gives de firemen news,
Couldn' make steam for de fire in de flues.
         Stow'n' sugar in de hull below, &c.

"Cap'n on de biler deck, a scratchin' of his head,
Hollers to de deck hand to heave de larbo'rd lead.
         Stow'n' sugar in de hull below, &c.

*   *   *   *   *   *   *   *

Perhaps the prettiest of all these songs is "The Wandering Steamboatman," which, like many other roustabout songs, rather frankly illustrates the somewhat loose morality of the calling:

> I am a wandering steamboatman,
>   And far away from home;
> I fell in love with a pretty gal,
>   And she in love with me.
>
> She took me to her parlor
>   And cooled me with her fan;
> She whispered in her mother's ear:
>   "I love the steamboatman."

The mother entreats her daughter not to become engaged to the stevedore. "You know," she says, "that he is a steamboatman, and has a wife at New Orleans." But the steamboatman replies, with great nonchalance:

> If I've a wife at New Orleans
> I'm neither tied nor bound;
> And I'll forsake my New Orleans wife
> If you'll be truly mine.

Another very curious and decidedly immoral song is popular with the loose women of the "Rows." We can only give one stanza:

> I hev a roustabout for my man—
> Livin' with a white man for a sham,
>   Oh, leave me alone,
>   Leave me alone,
> I'd like you much better if you'd leave me alone.

But the most famous songs in vogue among the roustabouts is "Limber Jim," or "Shiloh." Very few know it all by heart, which is not wonderful when we consider that it requires something like twenty minutes to sing "Limber Jim" from beginning to end, and that the whole song, if printed in full, would fill two columns of the Commercial. The only person in the city who can sing the song through, we believe, is a colored laborer living near Sixth and Culvert streets, who "run on the river" for years, and acquired so much of a reputation by singing "Limber Jim," that he has been nicknamed after the mythical individual aforesaid, and is now known by no other name. He keeps a little resort in Bucktown, which is known as "Limber Jim's," and has a fair reputation for one dwelling in that locality. Jim very good-naturedly sang the song for us a few nights ago, and we took down some of the most striking verses for the benefit of our readers. The air is wonderfully quick and lively, and the chorus is quite exciting. The leading singer sings the whole song, excepting the chorus, "Shiloh," which dissyllable is generally chanted by twenty or thirty voices of abysmal depth at the same time with a sound like the roar of twenty Chinese gongs struck with tremendous force and precision. A great part of "Limber Jim" is very profane, and some of it not quite fit to print. We can give only about one-tenth part of it. The chorus is frequently accompanied with that wonderfully rapid slapping of thighs and hips known as "patting Juba."

Nigger an' a white man playing seven-up,
White man played an ace; an' nigger feared to take it up,
White man played ace an' nigger played a nine,
White man died, an' nigger went blind.

> Limber Jim,
> [All.] Shiloh!
> Talk it agin,
> [All.] Shiloh!
> Walk back in love,
> [All.] Shiloh!
> You turtle-dove,
> [All.] Shiloh!

Went down the ribber, couldn't get across;
Hopped on a rebel louse; thought 'twas a hoss,
Oh lor', gals, 't ain't no lie,
Lice in Camp Chase big enough to cry,—
> Limber Jim, &c.

Bridle up a rat, sir; saddle up a cat,
Please han' me down my Leghorn hat,
Went to see widow; widow warn't home;
Saw to her daughter,—she gave me honeycomb.
> Limber Jim, &c.

Jay-bird sittin' on a swinging limb,
Winked at me an' I winked at him,
Up with a rock an' struck him on the shin,
G—d d—n yer soul, don't wink agin.
                    Limber Jim, &c.

Some folks says that a rebel can't steal,
I found twenty in my corn-fiel',
Sich pullin' of shucks an' tearin' of corn!—
Nebber saw the like since I was born.
                    Limber Jim, &c.

John Morgan come to Danville and cut a mighty dash,
Las' time I saw him, he was under whip an' lash;
'Long come a rebel at a sweepin' pace,
Whar 're ye goin', Mr. Rebel? "I'm goin' to Camp Chase."
                    Limber Jim, &c.

Way beyond de sun and de moon,
White gal tole me I were too soon,
White gal tole me I come too soon,
An' nigger gal called me an ole d—d fool.
                    Limber Jim, &c.

Eighteen pennies hidden in a fence,
Cynthiana gals ain't got no sense;
Every time they go from home
Comb thar heads wid an ole jaw bone.
                    Limber Jim, &c.

Had a little wife an' didn' inten' to keep her;
Showed her a flatboat an' sent her down de ribber;
Head like a fodder-shock, mout like a shovel,
Put yerself wid yaller gal, put yerself in trouble.
                    Limber Jim, &c.

I went down to Dinah's house, Dinah was in bed,
Hoisted de window an' poked out her head;
T'rowed, an' I hit in her de eyeball,—bim;
"Walk back, Mr. Nigger; don't do dat agin."
                    Limber Jim, &c.

Gambling man in de railroad line,
Saved my ace an' played my nine;
If you want to know my name,
My name's High-low-jack-in-the-game.
> Limber Jim,
> Shiloh!
> Talk it agin,
> Shiloh!
> You dancing girl,
> Shiloh!
> Sure's you're born,
> Shiloh!

Grease my heel with butter in the fat,
I can talk to Limber Jim better'n dat.
> Limber Jim,
> Shiloh!
> Limber Jim,
> Shiloh!
> Walk back in love,
> Shiloh!
> My turtle dove,
> Shiloh!

Patting Juba—And you can't go yonder,
> Limber Jim!
> And you can't go yonder,
> Limber Jim!
> And you can't go-oo-o!

One fact worth mentioning about these negro singers is, that they can mimic the Irish accent to a degree of perfection which an American, Englishman or German could not hope to acquire. At the request of Patrolman Tighe and his partner, the same evening that we interviewed Limber Jim, a very dark mulatto, named Jim Delaney, sang for us in capital style that famous Irish ditty known as "The hat me fahther wor-re." Yet Jim, notwithstanding his name, has little or no Irish blood in his veins; nor has his companion, Jim Harris, who joined in the rollicking chorus:

> " 'Tis the raylics of ould dacency,
> The hat me fahther wor-r-re."

Jim Delaney would certainly make a reputation for Irish specialties in a minstrel troupe; his mimicry of Irish character is absolutely perfect, and he possesses a voice of great flexibility, depth and volume. He "runs" on the river.

On the southeast corner of Culvert and Sixth streets, opposite to the house in which we were thus entertained by Limber Jim and his friends, stands Kirk's building, now occupied jointly by Kirk and Ryan. Two stories beneath this building is now the most popular dance-house of the colored steamboatmen and their "girls." The building and lot belong to Kirk; but Ryan holds a lease on the basement and half of the upper building. Recently the landlord and the leaseholder had a falling out, and are at bitter enmity; but Ryan seems to have the upper hand in the matter, and is making considerable money from the roustabouts. He has closed up the old side entrance, admission to the ball-room being now obtainable only through the bar-room, and the payment of ten cents. A special policeman has been wisely hired by the proprietor to preserve order below, and the establishment is, generally speaking, well conducted for an establishment of the kind. The amount of patronage it receives depends almost wholly upon the condition of the river traffic; during the greater part of the week the attendance is somewhat slim, but when the New Orleans boats come in the place is crowded to overflowing. Beside the admittance fee of ten cents, an additional dime is charged to all the men for every set danced—the said dime to be expended in "treating partners." When the times are hard and money scarce, the girls often pay the fees for their men in order to make up sets.

With its unplastered and windowless limestone walls; sanded floor; ruined ceiling, half plank, half cracked plaster; a dingy black counter in one corner, and rude benches ranged along the walls, this dancing-room presented rather an outlandish aspect when we visited it. At the corner of the room opposite "the bar," a long bench was placed, with its face to the wall; and upon the back of this bench, with their feet inwardly reclining upon the seat, sat the musicians. A well-dressed, neatly-built mulatto picked the banjo, and a somewhat lighter colored musician led the music with a fiddle, which he played remarkably well and with great spirit. A short, stout negress, illy dressed, with a rather good-natured face and a bed shawl tied about her head, played the bass viol, and that with no inexperienced hand. This woman is known to the police as Anna Nun.

The dancers were in sooth a motley crew; the neat dresses of the girls strongly contrasting with the rags of the poorer roustabouts, some of whom were clad only in shirt, pants and shocking hats. Several wickedly handsome women were smoking stogies. Bill Williams, a good-natured black giant, who keeps a Bucktown saloon, acted for a while as Master of Ceremonies. George Moore, the colored Democrat who killed, last election day, the leader of a party who attacked his house, figured to advantage in the dance, possessing wonderful activity in spite of his heavy bulk. The best performer on the floor was a stumpy little roustabout named Jem Scott, who is a marvelous jig-dancer, and can waltz with a tumbler full of water on his head without spilling a drop. One-fourth of the women present were white, including two girls only about seventeen years old, but bearing physiognomical evidence of precocious vice. The best-looking girl in the room was a tall, lithe quadroon named Mary Brown, with auburn hair, gray eyes, a very fair skin, and an air of quiet innocence wholly at variance with her reputation. A short, supple mulatto girl, with a blue ribbon in her hair, who attracted considerable admiration, and was famous for dancing "breakdowns," had but recently served a term in the penitentiary for grand larceny. Another woman present, a gigantic negress, wearing a red plaid shawl, and remarkable for an immense head of frizzly hair, was, we were informed, one of the most adroit thieves known to the police. It was a favorite trick of hers to pick a pocket while dancing, and hide the stolen money in her hair.

"How many of those present do you suppose carry knives?" we asked Patrolman Tighe.

"All of them," was the reply. "All the men, and women, too, carry knives or razors; and many of them pistols as well. But they seldom quarrel, except about a girl. Their great vice is thieving; and the fights down here are generally brought about by white roughs who have no business in this part of town except crime."

The musicians struck up that weird, wild, lively air, known perhaps to many of our readers as the "Devil's Dream," and in which "the musical ghost of a cat chasing the spectral ghost of a rat" is represented by a succession of "miauls" and "squeaks" on the fiddle. The dancers danced a double quadrille, at first, silently and rapidly; but warming with the wild spirit of the music, leaped and shouted, swinging each other off the floor, and keeping time with a precision which shook the building in time to the music. The women, we noticed, almost invariably embraced the men about the neck in swinging, the men clasping them about the waist. Sometimes the men advancing leaped and crossed legs with a double shuffle, and with almost sightless rapidity. Then the music changed to an old Virginia reel, and the dancing changing likewise, presented the most grotesque spectacle imaginable. The dancing became wild; men patted juba and shouted, the negro women danced with the most fantastic grace, their bodies describing almost incredible curves forward and backward; limbs intertwined rapidly in a wrestle with each other and with the music; the room presented a tide of swaying bodies and tossing arms, and flying hair. The white female dancers seemed heavy, cumbersome, ungainly by contrast with their dark companions; the spirit of the music was not upon them; they were abnormal to the life about them. Once more the music changed—to some popular negro air, with the chorus—

> "Don't get weary,
> I'm goin' home."

The musicians began to sing; the dancers joined in; and the dance terminated with a roar of song, stamping of feet, "patting juba," shouting, laughing, reeling. Even the curious spectators involuntarily kept time with their feet; it was the very drunkenness of music, the intoxication of the dance. Amid such scenes does the roustabout find his heaven; and this heaven is certainly not to be despised.

The great dancing resort for steamboatmen used to be Pickett's, on Sausage Row; but year after year the river came up and flooded all the grimy saloons on the Rows, and, departing, left behind it alluvial deposits of yellow mud, and the Spirit of Rheumatic Dampness. So, about

two months ago, Pickett rented out his old quarters, partly
as a barber-shop, partly as a shooting-gallery, and moved
into the building, No. 91 Front street, between Ludlow
and Lawrence. He has had the whole building renovated
throughout, and painted the front very handsomely. The
basement on the river side is now used for a dancing-
room; but the room is very small, and will not accommo-
date half of the dancers who used to congregate in the
old building. The upper part of the building the old man
rents out to river men and their wives or mistresses, using
the second floor for a restaurant and dining-rooms, which
are very neatly fitted up. Whatever may have been the
old man's sins, Pickett has a heart full of unselfish charity
sufficient to cover them all. Year after year, through good
or ill-fortune, he has daily fed and maintained fifty or
sixty homeless and needy steamboatmen. Sometimes when
the river trade "looks up," and all the boats are running
on full time, some grateful levee hand repays his bene-
factor, but it is very seldom. And the old man never asks
for it or expects it; he only says: "Boys, when you want
to spend your money, spend it here." Although now very
old, and almost helpless from a rupture, Pickett has yet
but to rap on the counter of his saloon to enforce instantaneous quiet. The roustabouts will miss the old man
when he is gone—the warm corner to sleep in, the simple
but plentiful meal when out of a berth, and the rough
kindness of his customary answer to a worthless, hungry,
and shivering applicant for food and lodging, "G—d d—n
you, you don't deserve it; but come in and behave your-
self." The day is not far off when there will be great
mourning along the levee.

With the exception of Ryan's dance-house, and one
or two Bucktown lodging-houses, the roustabouts gen-

erally haunt the Rows, principally Sausage Row, from Broadway to Ludlow street. Rat Row, from Walnut to Main, is more especially the home of the white tramps and roustabouts. Here is situated the celebrated "Blazing Stump," otherwise called St. James Restaurant, which is kept by a Hollander, named Venneman. Venneman accommodates only white men, and endeavors to keep an orderly house; but the "Blazing Stump" must always remain a resort for thieves, burglars, and criminals of every description. The "Stump" is No. 13 Rat Row. No. 16 is a lodging house for colored roustabouts, kept by James Madison. No. 12 is a policy shop, although it pretends to be a saloon; and the business is so cunningly conducted that the police can not, without special privilege, succeed in closing up the business. No. 10, which used to be known as Buckner's, is another haunt for colored roustabouts. They have a pet crow attached to the establishment, which is very plucky, and can whip all the cats and dogs in the neighborhood. It waddles about on the sidewalk of sunny days, pecking fiercely at any stranger who meddles with it, but the moment it sees the patrolmen coming along the levee it runs into the house.

No. 7—Goodman's clothing store—is said to be a "fence." At the west end of the row is Captain Dilg's celebrated hostelry, a popular and hospitable house, frequented by pilots and the most respectable class of river men. At the eastern terminus of the row is the well known Alhambra saloon, a great resort for colored steamboatmen, where large profits are realized on cigars and whisky of the cheapest kind. The contractors who hire roustabouts frequently have a private understanding with the proprietor of some levee coffee-house or saloon, and always go there to pay off their hands. Then the first one treats,

then another, and so on until all the money just made by
a day's heavy labor is lying in the counter drawer, and
the roustabouts are helplessly boozy.

Of the two rows Sausage Row is perhaps the most famous. No. 1 is kept by old Barney Hodke, who has made
quite a reputation by keeping a perfectly orderly house
in a very disorderly neighborhood. No. 2 is Cottonbrook's
clothing store, *alias* the "American Clothing Store," whereof the proprietor is said to have made a fortune by selling
cheap clothing to the negro stevedores. No. 3 is Mrs.
Sweeney's saloon and boarding-house, an orderly establishment for the entertainment of river men. No. 4 is an
eating- and lodging-house for roustabouts, kept by Frank
Fortner, a white man. No. 6 is a barber-shop for colored
folks, with a clothing-store next to it. No. 7 is a house of
ill-fame, kept by a white woman, Mary Pearl, who boards
several unfortunate white girls. This is a great resort for
colored men.

No. 8 is Maggie Sperlock's. Maggie has another saloon in Bucktown. She is a very fat and kind-hearted old
mulatto woman, who is bringing up half a dozen illegiti-
mate children, abandoned by their parents. One of these,
a very pretty boy, is said to be the son of a white lady,
who moves in good society, by a colored man.

No. 9 is now Chris. Meyer's; it was known as "Schwabe
Kate's" when Meyer's wife lived. This is the great resort
for German tramps.

Next in order comes a barber-shop and shooting-
gallery—"Long Branch" and "Saratoga." These used to
be occupied by Pickett.

A few doors east of this is Chas. Redman's saloon,
kept by a crippled soldier. This is another great roustabout haunt, where robberies are occasionally committed.
And a little further east is Pickett's new hotel. On these

two rows Officers Brazil and Knox have made no less than two hundred and fifty-six arrests during the past two years. The most troublesome element is, of course, among the white tramps.

A number of the colored river men are adroit thieves; these will work two or three months and then "lay off" until all their money has found its way to whisky-shops and brothels. The little clothing and shoe stores along the levee are almost daily robbed of some articles by such fellows, who excel in ingenious confidence dodges. A levee hand with extinct cigar will, for example, walk into a shoe shop with a "Say, bohss, giv a fellah a light." While the "bohss" is giving a light to the visitor, who always takes care to stand between the proprietor and the doorway, a confederate sneaks off with a pair of shoes. A fellow called "China Robinson," who hangs about Madison's, is said to be famous at such tricks. The police officers, however, will not allow any known sluggard or thief to loaf about the levee for more than thirty days without employment. There is always something to do for those who wish to do it, and roustabouts who persist in idleness and dirt, after one or two friendly warnings, get sent to the Work-house.

Half of the colored 'longshoremen used at one time to wear only a coat and pants, winter and summer; but now they are a little more careful of themselves, and fearful of being sent to the Work-house to be cleaned up. Consequently, when Officer Brazil finds a very ragged and dirty specimen of levee life on the Row, he has seldom occasion to warn him more than once to buy himself a shirt and a change of garments.

Generally speaking, the women give very little trouble. Some of the white girls now living in Pickett's barracks or in Bucktown brothels are of respectable parentage.

Two of the most notorious are sisters, who have a sad history. They are yet rather handsome. All these women are morphine eaters, and their greatest dread is to be sent to the Work-house, and being thus deprived of this stimulant. Some who were sent to the Work-house, we were told, had died there from want of it. The white girls of the Row soon die, however, under any circumstances; their lives are often fairly burnt out with poisonous whisky and reckless dissipation before they have haunted the levee more than two or three years. After a fashion, the roustabouts treat their women kindly, with a rough good nature that is peculiar to them; many of the women are really married. But faithfulness to a roustabout husband is considered quite an impossible virtue on the levee. The stevedores are mostly too improvident and too lazy to support their "gals." While the men are off on a trip, a girl will always talk about what she will be able to buy "when my man comes back—if he has any money." When the lover does come back, sometimes after a month's absence, he will perhaps present his "gal" with fifty cents, or at most a dollar, and thinks he has done generously by her. We are speaking in general terms, of course, and alluding to the mass of the colored roustabouts who "run on the river" all their lives, and have no other calling. It is needless to say that there are thrifty and industrious stevedores who support their families well, and will finally leave the river for some more lucrative employment.

Such is a glimpse of roustabout life. They know of no other life; they can understand no other pleasures. Their whole existence is one vision of anticipated animal pleasure or of animal misery; of giant toil under the fervid summer sun; of toil under the icy glare of the winter moon; of fiery drinks and drunken dreams; of the madness of music and the intoxication of fantastic dances; of white and dark mistresses awaiting their coming at the levees, with waving of brightly colored garments; of the deep music of the great steam whistles; of the torch-basket fires redly dancing upon the purple water, the white stars sailing overhead, the passing lights of well known cabins along the dark river banks, and the mighty panting of the iron heart of the great vessel, bearing them day after day and night after night to fresh scenes of human frailty, and nearer to that Dim Levee slope, where weird boats ever discharge ghostly freight, and depart empty.

Black Varieties

THE ATTRACTIVE novelty of theatricals at old Pickett's tavern, on the levee, by real negro minstrels, with amateur dancing performances by roustabouts and their "girls," has already created considerable interest in quarters where one would perhaps least expect to find it; and the patrolmen of the Row nightly escort fashionably dressed white strangers to No. 91 Front street. The theater has two entrances, one through the neat, spotlessly clean bar-room on the Front street side, the other from the sidewalk on the river side. The theater is also the ball-room; and when the ancient clock behind the black bar in the corner announces in senile, metallically-husky tones the hour of 12, the footlights are extinguished, the seats cleared away, and the audience quickly form into picturesque sets for wild dances.

It is a long, low room, with a staircase at the southwest corner, ascending to the saloon above; an unplastered ceiling of clean white pine plank, resembling an inverted section of steamboat deck, a black wooden bar at the southeast corner, and rude wooden benches of unpainted plank arranged along the walls and across the room from the bar to the stage. This stage consists of a wooden platform, elevated about a yard from the floor; and the little room under the staircase at the left side serves as the green-room. Tallow dips, placed about a foot apart, serve for footlights. Strips of white muslin sewed together form the curtains, which are attached by rings to a metal rod in the ceiling, and open and close much after the manner of the curtains of an old-fashioned, four-posted bedstead. These curtains were made by a mild-mannered brown girl called Annie, remarkable for deep, dark eyes, light, wavy hair, and wonderful curves of mouth, chin and neck; but poor Annie is no better than she ought to be, and loves to smoke a great, black, brier-root pipe.

Ere the curtain rose we found it extremely interesting to glance over the motley audience, largely made up of women less fair, but not less frail than Annie.

A sharp-faced Irish girl, with long fawn-colored hair and hard gray eyes; a pretty and ruddy-faced young white woman, very neatly built and fashionably dressed, the wife of a colored bar-keeper; a white brunette, with unpleasantly deep-set black eyes and long curly hair, who feigns to have colored blood in her veins; a newly arrived white blonde, who last week followed a roustabout hither from Ironton through some strange and vain infatuation; the notorious Adams sisters; a young Cincinnati woman of evil repute, whose parents live but a few squares up town, and have not for years exchanged word or look with their daughter, though she almost daily passes by the old home; and one Gretchen-faced woman, with rather regular features and fair hair, who has lately deserted a good home at Portsmouth to become the mistress of a stevedore—these

comprised the white women present. Excepting the bar-
keeper's little white wife, they evidently preferred to sit
togther. But the picturesqueness of the spectacle was rendered all the more striking by the contrast.

Every conceivable hue possible to the human skin
might be studied in the dense and motley throng that filled
the hall. There were full-blooded black women, solidly
built, who were smoking stogies, and wore handkerchiefs
of divers colors twined about their curly pates, after the
old Southern fashion. Some of these were evidently too
poor to own a whole dress, and appeared in petticoat
and calico waist alone; but the waists had been carefully
patched and washed, and the white petticoats were spotlessly clean and crisp with starch. Others were remarkably well dressed—excepting their ornaments, which were
frequently of a character calculated to provoke a smile.
One little negro woman had a flat locket with a brilliantly-
colored picture painted on it, and at least six inches in
diameter, suspended from her ebon neck by a golden
chain. Gold or imitation, yellow and glittering, flashed
everywhere in ear pendants against dusky cheeks, in massive rings upon strong black hands, in fair chains coiling
about brown necks or clasping bare brown arms.

It is a mystery how many of these women, who can
not afford to buy two dresses, or who have to borrow de-
cent attire to go out of doors, can refuse to part with their
jewelry in almost any extremity, but we have been reliably
assured that such is the case. As a rule these levee girls
do not invest in bogus jewelry. It was curious to observe
the contrast of physical characteristics among the lighter-
hued women; girls with almost fair skins frequently possessing wooly hair; dark mulattoes on the contrary often
having light, floating, wavy locks. One mulatto girl pres-

ent wore her own hair—frizzly and thick as the mane of a
Shetland pony—flowing down to her waist in gipsy style.
Where turbans were not worn among the fairer skinned,
the hair was generally confined with a colored ribbon. At
least three-fourths of the audience were women, and of
these one-third, perhaps, were smoking—several of the
white girls were chewing. Of the men present, the greater
number were roustabouts, in patched attire, often of the
most fantastic description. Four musicians played lively
old-time tunes before the stage, and through the half-open
door at the other end of the theater glimpses were visible
of an expanse of purple, star-studded sky, a more deeply
purple expanse of rippling river, the dark rolling outline
of the Kentucky hills, and a long line of yellow points of
light, scattered along the curving shore as far as the eye
could reach. From without, the cool, sweet river air occasionally crept in by gentle breaths, and from within,
the dim light of trembling candle-flame, the blue wreaths
of heavy tobacco smoke, the sound of vociferous laughter
and the notes of wild music, all floated out together into
the white moonlight.

The little stage curtain rose, or, rather, parted, upon
a scene originally ludicrous in itself, which evoked a shout
of mingled glee and amusement from the expectant audience. The six performers were, with one exception, very
dark men, with pronounced negro features; but they had
exaggerated their natural physiognomical characteristics
by a lavish expenditure of burnt cork and paint. The
mouths of the end-men grinned from ear to ear; their eyes
appeared monstrous, and their attire could not have been
done justice to by any ordinary play-bill artist. It was a
capital get up in its line, such as white minstrels could
hardly hope to equal. The three principal performers

were professionals from Louisville. The right end man
had a tambourine with a silver rim, which he unfortunately smashed during the evening by knocking it against his
pate, and as a tambourine performer he can not have many
white rivals, tapping the instrument against his hand,
elbow, knee, head, foot, with a rapidity which almost de-
fied the eye to follow it.

After the first musical performance minstrel jokes
were in order, including odd conundrums, "hits" at the
patrolmen, and miscellaneous jokes of a humorous, but
always innocent description. Here is a specimen:

"How dy'e feel to-night, Mr. Royal?"

"I feel's as if I was in de clouds; an' angels pouring
'lasses all over me."

"Well, Mr. Royal, I want to prepose a kolumdrum to
you. Kin you spell 'blind pig' with two letters?"

"Cou'se I kin. Blind pig?—let's see!—pig? P-g, pig."

"Wrong, sir; wrong. B-l-i-n-d, blind, p-i-g, pig—blind
pig. Thar's an 'i' in pig, an' you left out the eye."

"But if he's got an eye, he can't be a blind pig."
[Roars of laughter.]

"Hev' you got a wife, Mr. Moore?"

"Yes."

"Isn't it sweet to hev' a nice little wife?"

"Yes."

"When you git up in de morning she kin give you a
s-t-r-o-n-g cup of coffee."

"Yes."

"An' give you nice, strong butter?"

"No; not strong butter."

"An' give you a nice, strong hug?"

"Yes."

"An' kiss you at the door, and say, 'By-by, baby; dream
of me?'"

"Yes."

"An' when y'ar just gone out the front way, open de back door an' let a great big black niggar in de back way?"

Then they sung a song, with a roaring chorus, called "Cahve de Possum," after which came more jokes, and then a most comical scene—really the best performance of the evening—between two men, one attired as a woman, with an enormously exaggerated "pull-back," and the other costumed as a journeyman whitewasher. The effects of this scene upon the audience was extremely interesting. The women not only laughed but screamed and leaped in their seats, to fall back and laugh till the tears ran down their cheeks. A well built young black woman named Lucy Mason, whose face still bore the scars of a recent razor-slash, then came upon the stage, attired in a short petticoat with scalloped edges; striped stockings, which displayed a pair of solid, well-turned legs; and boy's brogans. She danced a break-down very fairly, and was several times called out. Then a little roustabout, from New Orleans, danced a jig; and the performance closed with a lengthy but very comical extravaganza entitled "Damon and Pythias." To the curious visitor, however, the merits of the performance, although an excellent one, was far less entertaining than the spectacle of the enjoyment which it occasioned—the screams of laughter and futile stuffing of handkerchiefs in laughing mouths, the tears of merriment, the innocent appreciation of the most trivial joke, the stamping of feet and leaping, and clapping of hands— a very extravaganza of cachination.

Midnight twanged out from the ancient clock, laughter was heard only in occasional chuckles, a roustabout extinguished the footlights with his weatherbeaten hat, the bar became thronged with dusky drinkers, and the musicians put their instruments by. Then the room suddenly vibrated in every fiber of its pine-planking to a long, deeply swelling sound, which suddenly hushed the chatter like a charm. Half of the hearts in the room beat a little faster—hearts well trained to recognize the Voices of the River; and the sound grew stronger and sweeter, like an unbroken roll of soft, rich, deep thunder. "The Wildwood," shouted a score of voices at once, and the throng rushed out on the levee to watch the great white boat steaming up in the white moonlight, with a weird train of wreathing smoke behind her, and dark lovers of swarthy levee girls on board.

"Butler's"

On the east side of Broadway, between Sixth and New streets, stands a hideous little frame building about fifteen feet high, some four yards back from the sidewalk. Its grimy ugliness is further enhanced by a deep and darksome porch, supported by black and battered beams; and the absence of lighted windows of an evening, combined with the ominous quiet of its immediate surroundings, conjures up blood-curdling visions of those lonesome inns in the Hartz Mountains we have all read of, as children, in "Tales of Horror." The very neighborhood is a most unpleasant one to pass through of a winter's night—full of fifth-class negro brothels, dark door-ways wherein sable harlots watch for victims, suspicious-looking alleys echoing with sounds of brutal brawl or drunken riot, dilapidated tenement houses, and architectural monstrosities of the most abnormal and abominable description. With such known surroundings, a passer-by would probably regard "Butler's" as a den of infamy unutterable, the resort of harlots, thieves and negro outlaws. But this is far from being the truth. In fact that frightful hovel is considered by the poorer and blacker classes of colored people as quite a respectable hotel and restaurant. A rough levee-hand never considers that he has done his duty by his girl unless he has taken her for an evening to "Butler's"—as this place is called—and treated her to fish and eggs, or a pig's foot and some liquid concoction which it would be calumnious to call whisky or wine. "Butler's," in its way, is probably by far the most popular place in the negro quarters. Butler insists upon good order in his establishment, and sways its denizens with a will stronger than his own muscles of iron. Suppose we take a peep into "Butler's."

On opening the door you are saluted with a whiff of hot air, redolent of multifarious foulnesses—the stench of saliva squirted upon a red-hot stove, the odor of villainous tobacco, the familiar smell of salt fish, the sickening aroma of bad breaths qualified with forty-rod whisky, and one or two other stinks which it would not be decorous to name. By the time your lungs have temporarily recovered from this hideous shock you have discovered that the whole area occupied by "Butler's" does not exceed fifteen by fifteen. The ceiling is about eight feet high. Before the door stands a long, high wooden screen, situated so as to shut out from the street all view of the dingy room and its occupants. In the northeast corner stands an immense ice-chest; and the space behind the screen is filled up by rickety wooden chairs, black with age, and polished by perpetual use. Athletic negroes, mostly of the blackest hue; one or two gigantic mulattoes with a most villainous expression of countenance, and their girls, are seated behind the screen, eating and drinking. The prettiest class of colored girl, the supple, lithe quadroon or octoroon will seldom be found here—probably for the reason that the average of pretty colored girls are generally virtuous. Hideous negresses and vicious dark-brown women are, however, plentiful at "Butler's" during the early part of the evening. To the right stands the bar, long and well-worn, with the sideboard behind covered with ranges of glasses and bottles, rising tier upon tier, to be reflected in a greasy mirror with a battered frame, and crowned with deer's antlers. Here sits in weird state, winking sapiently with solemn yellow eyes, the guardian-genius of the place. Not Butler himself, the dark-featured fellow who looks as though he might have been just imported from Ashantee, but a bird. Fancy a bird (the brightest and purest of all God's creatures is a soft-plumaged, bead-eyed bird) in such a place! But this is not a white-bosomed dove, a silver-throated canary, or a merry mocking-bird. It is a foul and unclean bird—the bird whose flesh Moses forbade the children of Israel to eat—the bird whose brothers are the ravens and buzzards that fatten upon the crawling flesh of things dead—the bird that abhors the pure light of day—*the owl*. Verily a most ill-omened and foul bird, well fitted to dwell in so hideous a place. All night he watches from the mirror-frame, with flaming yellow eyes, the ugly sights about him, and inhales the noisome exhalations of the apartment.

When midnight comes the harlots depart, and Butler's lodgers haggle for places to rest. They have mostly had their suppers—three hard-boiled eggs for a dime, a fifteen-cent fish or a ten-cent pig's-foot on a slice of stale

rye bread. The ice-chest brings forty-five cents a night
to its proprietor as a bunk, being rented out to three at
fifteen cents a-piece. Two benches are rented out at fifteen
cents each, and those who wish to sleep in chairs pay a
dime for the night. Then the lights are extinguished, and
the flaming eyes of the owl become phosphorescently visible through the noisome gloom.

Auntie Porter

SOMETIMES children are born on the levee—children of poor outcast women, to whom maternity is rather a curse than a blessing. It seems somewhat odd, indeed, that children should be born amid such scenes of reckless shame and reeking sin, but many a little one has first opened its great black eyes to the light in some one of those gloomy and dilapidated levee buildings, from whose windows the dark women wave gaily-hued handkerchiefs to departing vessels. Brown, vigorous, bright-eyed pretty waifs these infants often are; unscathed by the sin of their birth, and exhibiting even in earliest babyhood the quaintest cunning and funniest merriment imaginable. But the little ones are seldom long nursed by their own mothers; and the cry of a child is rarely heard along the Rows in the night stillness. So, in view of the fact that these babies mostly inherit very vigorous constitutions, one naturally inquires with an ominous and horrified expression: "What becomes of them?"

Well, there is a door and a heart ever open for the little waifs—a little door that is very old and ugly and weak; and a great heart, that is also very old—indeed, much older, but still brave and warm and true. And this open door and open heart may be found in the center of the negro quarter called Bucktown.

If curiosity should ever prompt you to visit the corner of Sixth and Culvert streets, ask some one of the tall, dark, turbaned women who haunt the doors of Kirk's underground dance-house to tell you where "Auntie Porter" lives. Then you will be directed to the rear of Kirk's building, where the ground is yellow and soft, and the noisome air black with flies; and where you will see a wretched little hamlet of sooty frame cottages whose grimy plank walls afford a strange contrast to the snowy freight of overburthened clothes-lines extending in every direction. Auntie Porter lives in the lowliest and most ancient of all these inky-colored frames,—the best of foundling hospitals, nevertheless, for the Children of the Levee. And Auntie herself may generally be seen there, seated by her door, probably smoking her old-fashioned briar-root pipe.

Auntie is very old; she has seen her eighty-second year. But she is still strong and hearty, though age has dimmed her eyes and taught her hands to tremble a little, when she is filling that old black pipe. Her dark-brown face is cast in the most strongly marked African mold; her lips are very large and long; her nostrils very flat; her cheek-bones very high; her broad face is weirdly wrinkled. It would be a very ugly face but for the relief of the kindliest of motherly smiles, and the incessant twinkle of good-humored fun in her half-blind eyes. That smile and look have won the love of motherless little ones more numerous, perhaps, than even the years of Auntie Porter. A great white turban and a huge rusty-colored wrapper lend Auntie quite a picturesque appearance. Her little house is dingy and dark, and swarms with flies; her furniture is so old that one wonders why the chairs and tables do not fall to pieces; and the floor of the rickety building squeals and groans under her feet. But she is very contented and happy, and complains of nothing, even when the rains beat through the roof or a northeaster shrieks through the cracks of the shuddering doors and windows.

From time to time some levee girl brings her baby to Auntie Porter, and abandons it forever, to return to the delirious revelry of the Row, with its drunken passion and wild music and weird debauch. Generally she promises to pay twenty-five or fifty cents a week for the baby's board, and almost always forgets to keep the promise. But Auntie cares little for that. "I becomes 'tached to de little ones," she says, "and kent give 'em up." She has successfully "raised" no less than nineteen of these motherless babes, besides having nursed a great number who died early, despite the tenderest care. Some of her foundlings have grown up to manhood and womanhood; some are doing well in other cities; some are running on the river; some have gone back to the wild life amid which they were born.

One fine tawny lad still visits his old foster-mother, when the boats come up from New Orleans, and this one always brings her half of his wages.

Auntie used once to be able to support her little ones well, when she was younger and stronger, and could work hard for them, but now she is getting too old to work. She chiefly manages to live only by boarding some poor negro longshoremen, and once in a while even this resource fails her, for her boarders are men who rove from city to city, and know by heart all the levee haunts on the Ohio and Mississippi. Then Auntie sometimes feels troubled, not for herself, but for the little ones—two of whom, a boy and girl, she is now nursing. But she never long wants friends, for even the roughest and wickedest women in Bucktown will contribute a mite to help her, and, if they lack the mite, will beg food for her and the children.

You may sometimes see her of a summer evening, when the fire-flies are flashing over the marshy ground before her cottage, sitting at her door with a child on either knee, smiling fondly upon them with her half-blind eyes, trying to hum to them snatches of old slave songs and queer, wild hymns; whispering soft admonitions to them, framed according to her old-fashioned faith; or telling strange stories of a strange land of which men know nothing, yet toward which all men forever travel. And it may come to pass, long after Auntie also shall have traveled silently thither, that some dim night, a powerful and passionate man, with arm uplifted for a deed darker than the Shadows of the Levee, shall feel his heart falter as there comes back to him a memory-echo of some wild slave hymn, which, during the well nigh forgotten years of his childhood, an aged and wrinkled negress once sang to him with kindly tears in her half-blind eyes.

The Rising of the Waters

BETWEEN THE hours of 8 A.M. and 5 P.M. yesterday the river rose thirty-five inches. Both of the Rows were under water early in the day, and the steamboat Minnie was paddling about where cargoes had been discharged but a few days ago. During the afternoon she was busy moving the wharfboats to higher ground.

The habitants of the Rows had received timely warning of the coming flood, but they managed to escape barely in time, as few anticipated the rapidity of the rise. Pickett prepared early Tuesday afternoon for the inundation, having had considerable experience beforehand in the matter of floods and storms. There was not much to remove in the dance-house, the furniture consisting chiefly of benches strongly riveted into the floor, a few tables for the banjo-players, and the counter with its fixings. The latter were removed, and the poor "hustlers," or homeless roustabouts, who had been quartered of nights in the basement, and supported during the hard times by the charity of "Old Pap," were kindly furnished with free lodging in

Pickett's boarding-house, up stairs. Old Maggie Sperlock succeeded in removing her household goods just before daybreak, but scarcely in time to escape a cold bath. Long Branch, the shooting gallery and the barber shops, were vacated only at the last moment. "Saratoga" had been vacated two days before, when its proprietor, Charley Redman, died in the Hospital. The levee people intended to hold a wake over the body, but the flood came before the wake could be held. According to the superstitions of the Row, therefore, the levee will be forever haunted by the poor fellow's ghost.

On the Lower Row the flood drove out all the basement tenants at an almost equally early hour. The Alhambra or Yellowhammer and the Break-o'-Day Saloon were vacated early in the morning, but not before the water was washing the threshholds. The proprietor of the "Break-o'-Day," which used to be Chris. Dilg's, was the principal victim of the watery cataclysm. He had been filling his big cellars with river ice for weeks past; and had hired many wagons and horses and roustabouts to remove the ice to his place of business. Several parties warned the old gentleman that the Row would be flooded, and that his ice would ere long be floating in muddy water, but he always answered, "Guess not, I know what I'm doing." After he had piled up tons upon tons in his cellar, the flood came with a vengeance, and the cellar on the corner of Walnut street and the levee, was one of the first to be filled. The "Blazing Stump" vomited forth its crowd of tramps and bummers before daylight, most of whom took refuge at a saloon on East Front street. One old, crippled fellow, who had paid his last quarter for board and lodging, insisted, during the forenoon, on wading, or rather trying to wade, back to the Stump. He was followed by a crowd of delighted urchins, who fondly hoped to witness a drowning sensation, but those watchful officers, Brazil and Knox, spoiled the fun by collaring the crazy cripple and thus saving him from a watery grave. He vowed angrily that he was "not going to be cheated of his last cent by the —— river," and was again, about half an hour later, detected in the attempt to return. So the officer had to lock him up for safe-keeping at the Hammond Street Police Station.

The proprietors of the junk-shops, "fences" and the few clothing-stores on the Rows were sharp enough to move out on Tuesday. Jot, the Voodoo, was not compelled to move until Wednesday noon, his den opening on the Front street side, and running back only half-way to Rat Row. He either hired or compelled a certain vigorous roustabout to help him in moving. The said roustabout went to work in great fear and trembling, standing on the sidewalk above the cellar opening, and taking articles of furniture, &c., from Jot's outstretched hands below. At last the roustabout carelessly exclaimed "All right" before he had got a good hold upon a kitchen safe which Jot was holding up to him. The safe fell with a crash upon the Voodoo's bald head, and a tempest of maledictions arose from the blackness beneath, mingled with awful objurgations in an unknown tongue. The roustabout did not stay to make many apologies, but fled wildly toward the east.

By 4 o'clock in the afternoon the white sides of the steamboats were pressing against the massive "guards" bordering the sidewalks of the Rows, and the river was rolling with a deep hum, which could be heard distinctly above all other sounds of the levee. Before 5 o'clock it had become impossible for boats to pass under the bridge.

Crowds assembled upon the slope to watch the visible broadening of the yellow stream, and enterprising fakirs, perched upon piles of cargo, made money rapidly by the exhibition of "ring tricks."

Probably the coming of the flood was not much regretted by the Children of the Levee, who now rejoice in the prospects of river traffic. No such misery as that which haunted the Rows this winter ever visited the levee before. During the long weeks that the river lay bound by frost the poor stevedores lacked often the very necessaries of life. Incapable of regarding money, except as a medium for pleasure, they had made no provision for the terrible winter, and the results of hunger among the dwellers along the Upper Row became shocking. The poor fellows gathered about the stoves in the cheerless dance-houses, gaunt, famished, miserable and silent. Their general feeling of helpless misery—the cruel hunger gnawing at their vitals— produced upon these naturally cheerful, childish natures the signs of such distress as one sees in little dumb animals starving for food. They scarcely moved or spoke, and the dropping of a pin might have been heard with unpleasant distinctness in their famishing assemblies. But this sad condition of things could not last long. Pickett, who has really made no money whatever since the commencement of cold weather, soon sent word to the poor fellows that so long as his means held out, they should not want for food or a warm corner to sleep in. The bighearted old man bought food when it could be bought, begged it from the slaughter-houses when it could not be bought, and his cooks were before long busily at work all day in the cosy little kitchen of the boarding-house preparing soups and cheap but substantial dishes for the hungry folks. At night they always had a warm room to sleep in; and no negro riverman asked lodging from "Old Pap" without hearing the cheery answer, "Of course, child; come in, come in, and eat all you can." Pickett has probably given more charity this winter than even the Bethel; and, be it observed, at a heavy loss to himself. "I sometimes feel the boys are ungrateful," says the old man, "because they don't try to help me when they can. If you are hungry and I give you food, and you see me trying to lift one end of a beam, you'd naturally try to help me, because you'd think of how I'd helped you. But these boys won't. Still, I can't blame them. It isn't their nature to feel grateful long, because they are ignorant and thoughtless. They don't think long about anything. They're just like so many children."

Some charitable soul, who heard how "hard up" the poor colored men were, sent down to the Row, a few weeks ago, a big basket of meat and provisions. Every hungry stevedore had one solid meal that day, and everybody was happy. They took off their shoes and played at "circus" and lcap-frog, in the excess of their joy.

But when the ice broke, and the steamboats whistled once more, and the river surface became alive with the heaving and gliding of the pale ice, the Row gave vent to a burst of noisy joy which must have been plainly heard on the Kentucky shore. Women and men all rushed out of doors, cheered, shouted, waved hats and turbans, and danced with delight; for the crashing and booming of the broken ice promised work for all, money, and the merriment of dancing and drinking. Some even cried with joy, and wandered about with tears on their cheeks.

Genius Loci

You may have occasionally noticed on the east side of
Broadway, near Seventh street, a certain ugly little building, with bulging sides from which warped planks pro-
trude at intervals like the ribs of something starved, and
a floor prone to utter dying groans when trodden upon.
It has a decayed porch, which rises to the eaves of the
sooty roof, a ruined fence, and a couple of hungry-looking
trees, which seem anxious to force their gnarled arms
through the bar-room window in a grotesque effort to ap-
pease their thirst larceniously. From the open door floats
out of nights an odor of dried mackerel and stale beer—a
most ancient and fish-like smell—together with the tingle-
tan-tang-tangle of a banjo, and sometimes the jovial re-
frain—

"I'm Rag-a-back Sam.,
And I don't care a d—n,
Fur I sooner be a nigger dan a poor white man."

In the days of its celebrity as a resort for levee laborers and steamboatmen, this squalid-visaged place was known as Buckner's. That was five years ago, before Jim Buckner removed his Lares and Penates from the western boundary of Bucktown to No. 10 Sausage Row, where he unfortunately died one afternoon, just as the Golden City was steaming up to the levee with a large and thirsty colored crew. They burnt seventy-five cents' worth of tallow dips in the dead-room, and sang quaint ditties all night lest the good soul might come back again; after which business went on as usual at No. 10 Sausage Row.

The fame of Buckner's Broadway saloon, and subsequently of his public house on Sausage Row, was certainly attributable to something more original than the dried mackerel and blue-lightning whisky. Perhaps they owed much of their celebrity to their very peculiar *genii loci—genii* of a character somewhat in harmony with the

half-weird night life of the roustabout haunts, but assuredly ill-omened according to all popular superstition.
Perched upon the top of a long antiquated mirror, which
reflected the figures of the dancers within the Broadway
saloon, there sat night after night, in the old times, a small,
yellow-eyed owl, which calmly watched the revels below
until faint blue tints of early day stole through the broken
window-shutters. Some cunning hand had enabled him to
articulate sounds of human speech, by dissecting his little
tongue; and he became learned in the lore of Evil as one
of the goblin birds that hover over the orgiastic furies of
Walpurgis Night. Sitting directly in the angular shadow
which the inclined mirror flung up to the ceiling, his eyes
seemed to flare like infernal topazes; and between the
intervals of the music he ever solemnly devoted the souls
and hearts of the dancers to ceaseless torment in that bot-
tomless abyss, where the worm dieth not, and the fire is
not extinguished. At last the objurgating owl suddenly
and inexplicably disappeared.

"Lor' knows what becomed ob dat owl," observed
Banjo Jim, one day, when an inquisitive friend was making inquiries.

"De Lor' don'no nuffin 'bout dat yar owl," growled
Voodoo Jot: "on'y de debbil—*he* knows what am becomed
ob dat owl."

And from that time there ceased to exist any strong
doubt as to the fate of this spectral *genius loci*.

The owl vanished from mortal view before Buckner
"moved" down to the levee, but the place did not remain
long without its familiar *Daemon*. To the first *genius loci*
almost immediately succeeded another feathered goblin,
less weird, doubtless, than his predecessor, but yet even
more ill-omened—a great, gaunt, ghastly crow! Where that

crow came from we shall not attempt to say; the mystery of "Sam's" appearance had best be left to the warlock Jot for explanation.

Well, Buckner finally "moved down" to the levee, taking Sam with him, and passed away one summer evening. Sam remained at No. 10, occasionally pecking and pulling the poor piece of dusty crape that hung to the broken door-knob; or wandering about the place in a sad, aimless way, as though looking for Somebody who would never come back. When Willis reopened the business he took Sam away, although the bird fought savagely and uttered odd guttural sounds, as of one in pain. Willis was then carrying on business at two saloons, Buckner's old place on Broadway and No. 10 Sausage Row; and Sam was taken to the old house. There he drooped and refused to eat and pulled his feathers out, until one day he managed to escape from the bar-room and wandered down Broadway toward the levee. "Perhaps," said Willis, after they had caught the fugitive, "Sam wants to go back to No. 10."

So they brought him back to the levee, where the white boats were moving in and out, singing their deep steam songs, and they set Sam down by the weather-stained door, from which the fluttering fragments of crape, all gray with levee dust had been taken away. Sam saw the brown river, the smoke-breathing boats, and the cargo-bearing gangs of roustabouts singing the old songs of slavery, the heavy wagons lumbering through a fog of dust below, and the long span of the suspension bridge shadowing the broad water—and he laughed! It was the first time any one had heard Sam laugh, and a very queer laugh it was—deep, and guttural, and sinister, but withal bearing a mocking resemblance to the "Kee-yah! kee-yah!" of roustabout mirth. And from that day Sam continued to laugh at intervals, growing fat as he laughed.

If Sam's merriment seemed a mimicry of negro laughter, his habits certainly seemed a mockery of levee morals. He lounged all day in bar-rooms, or loafed in front of their open doors; he sat upon the curbstone, or on a doorsill, or dozed on a sunny log. He sat up all night to watch games of cards or plantation dances; he wandered about the levee by moonlight; he mingled with rough and drunken crowds, and, strange to say, never got hurt. He soon showed that he had as good an eye for contrasts of gaudy color as any of the levee girls, and shared their fondness for amassing pretty little trinkets and foolish little trifles— bits of red and blue and scarlet ribbons, fragments of looking-glass, bright metal buttons, odds and ends of everything that glittered or gleamed.

At the same time it became observed that his sense of moral right was in some sort defective, and assuredly there were many poor souls on the levee who must have felt for him that sympathetic friendship which springs from fellowship in sin. He was a great thief; he stole from his master and from his master's customers; he devoted himself daily to the study of petit larceny, and he learned even to excel in pickpocketing. If a steamboatman left his jacket on the seat of a chair while playing cards, and the pockets of the garment were lying within Sam's reach, those pockets would be found empty at the conclusion of the game. If a nickel or a bit of silver change fell from the counter or the card-table, Sam had seized it and was gone before he could be arrested. He was most expert, however, as a "sneak-thief." More than once he has been known to "tap the till" of No. 10; and he has been a source of incessant terror to the Jewish storekeepers further up the Row, who sell second-hand knives and pistols and garments to the steamboatmen. He has even stolen bunches of keys from the keyholes of trunks and chests of drawers, and hidden them in empty beer kegs, by dropping them through the bunghole. He haunted the "fence" of old Goodman, a few doors east of No. 10, and purloined money and trinkets and bits of finery at brief intervals, despite all possible watchfulness.

It did not take long for the levee folk to find out that Sam was almost a stranger to physical fear. Dogs who once ventured within his reach never did so again; and no barefooted stevedore who once attempted to kick Sam out of his way ever cared to repeat the experiment. In fact, Sam discovered a special aversion for barefooted people, and the longshoremen soon dreaded to enter No. 10 without boots on. But probably from being a constant offender against good morals, Sam became something of a moral coward. He learned to dread the approach of a policeman, and the sight of a blue uniform with brass buttons always sufficed to put him to flight.

Any fine afternoon that you have time to wander down to the Levee, you may see the "ebony bird" hopping about the doorway of his domicile. You may walk up to him, he will not run from you; you may sit down on a sun-warmed log beside him, and he will take no notice of you. You can not make him go indoors, he would fight you to the bitter end if you tried it; but the moment Officers Brazil and Knox appear at the eastern end of Sausage Row, the little thief takes flight and hops under the swinging doors into the bar-room. And if you wait until the officers have passed by, you will see the cunning rascal poke his sharp head round the corner to see whether the police are gone away. If they happen to turn their heads.

Sam dives under the door again; if they do not look back, he returns to the sunlight.

Symbolic of the homeless life about him seems this little feathered roustabout, with his black complexion, his big saucy eyes, his uncouth laughter, his love of sunlight and somnolent laziness, his propensity to theft, and his awful respect for the police. He is the type of the reckless longshoremen; he is the Genius Loci.

There is only one human being who has earned this mateless bird's affection—the trim mulatto bar-keeper of No. 10, by whom he sometimes suffers himself to be caressed; and the caresses are always returned in an elfish way, with tender nibbling of fingers and low murmuring cries of pleasure, which suggest all sorts of fond names, for the creature speaks an almost intelligible tongue, many-syllabled and deep-sounding as the Voices of the River.

Happiest he seems when alone and unobserved, and at such times he laughs the mysterious, deep laugh that has made him an object of fear to the superstitious levee-folk. Early in the dawn, ere the Row awakens from its half-drunken sleep, he wanders down the slope, and laughs as he watches the gray change to yellow in the brightening East, and the yellow blend into the blue above through faint shades of emerald, and the sun slowly raise his shining face above the undulations of the hills.

But he laughs most of all in the night, while following the course of those pale green fires which haunt the darkness, and which some say mark the passing of ghostly wanderers. Perhaps Sam knows they are not fire-flies.

He has watched the rising and falling of the waters, the coming and passing away of homeless men, for seven years, and age has left no mark upon him. For the raven and the crow may live through the centuries.

He may still live and laugh when the levee has become as thickly grass-grown as a place of graves, and frogs hold their melancholy chorus where ten thousand tons of cargo were hourly unshipped of old—when the piers of the giant bridges are green with ancient moss, and the deep-echoing music of river traffic no longer awakens the phantom voices of the hills.

CHILDREN OF THE LEVEE, composed and printed in the University of Kentucky printing plant and bound by the C. J. Krehbiel Company of Cincinnati, was designed and illustrated by William K. Hubbell. The book is set in Linotype Baskerville and Ludlow Eusebius, printed on Beckett Text wove paper, and bound in paper and Holliston Roxite cloth.